W9-DFB-721

PLANTS & GARDENS
BROOKLYN BOTANIC GARDEN RECORD
HANDBOOK #81

This Handbook is a Special Printing of PLANTS & GARDENS, Vol. 32, No. 2

BONSAI FOR INDOORS

CONTENTS

Right to left: *Serissa foetida* 'Variegata', Calamondin and Rosemary
summering outdoors at BBG .... Elvin McDonald Cover
Among Our Contributors .... Inside Front Cover
Indoor Bonsai in Training .... *Arthur Orans, Gregg R. Wadleigh*   2
Letter from the Brooklyn Botanic Garden   3
Introduction .... *Constance T. Derderian*   4
Bonsai in the House .... *Ernesta* and *Fred Ballard*   5
Indoor Bonsai are Different .... *Warren P. Cooper* and *Jerald P. Stowell* 11
What Makes a Good Bonsai? .... *Mary P. Case* 12
A Bonsai Refresher .... *Constance T. Derderian* 14
Wiring .... *Constance T. Derderian* 18
A Window Case for Bonsai 22
Care—Preliminary Requirements .... *Edmond O. Moulin* 24
Pruning Can Make the Difference .... *John Yoshio Naka* 26
Bonsai Styles .... *Constance T. Derderian* 29
Illustrated Guide to Bonsai Styles .... *Frank Okamura* 30
Mame Bonsai .... *Doris W. Froning* 33
The Light Garden .... *Margery M. Craig* 35
Kingsville Dwarf Box and Serissa .... *Albert J. Lake* 38
Camellias and Gardenias .... *Lynn Perry Alstadt* 40
Ficus: The Ornamental Fig .... *J. Richard Bowen* 42
The Myrtle of the Ancients .... *Elizabeth N. Hume* 44
Herbs and Succulents .... *Eleanor C. Thatcher* 47
One Hundred Plants from A to Z .... *Constance T. Derderian* 50
Indoor Bonsai in the North .... *Sigmund Dreilinger* 60
Report From the Pacific Northwest .... *Jane Nelson* 63
Even Bonsai Growers Need a Vacation .... *Edmond O. Moulin* 64
Notes on Growing Bonsai in the Deep South
                          Winifred F. Glover and *Virginia Harvey* 65
Bonsai Books and Films from the Brooklyn Botanic Garden 67
Indoor Bonsai in South Florida .... *Virginia Nichols* 68
Indoor Bonsai in Hawaii .... *David Fukumoto* 71
Index 75

Staff for this issue:
CONSTANCE T. DERDERIAN, *Guest Editor*
FREDERICK MCGOURTY, JR., *Editor*
MARGARET E.B. JOYNER and MARJORIE J. DIETZ, *Associate Editors*
with the assistance of EDMOND O. MOULIN
and the Editorial Committee of the Brooklyn Botanic Garden
VIOLETTE CONNOLLY, *Secretary of Publications*
DONALD E. MOORE, *President, Brooklyn Botanic Garden*
ELIZABETH SCHOLTZ, *Vice President, Brooklyn Botanic Garden*

Plants and Gardens, Brooklyn Botanic Garden Record (ISSN 0362-5850) is published quarterly at 1000 Washington Ave., Brooklyn, N.Y. 11225, by the **Brooklyn Botanic Garden, Inc.** Second-class-postage paid at Brooklyn, N.Y., and at additional mailing offices. Subscriptions included in Botanic Garden membership dues ($20.00 per year), which includes newsletters and announcements. Copyright © 1953, 1989 by the Brooklyn Botanic Garden, Inc.
POSTMASTER: Send address changes to BROOKLYN BOTANIC GARDEN, Brooklyn, N.Y. 11225

Indoor bonsai in training—
the on-going challenge.

Arthur Orans

Beautiful structure for beginning bonsai. This Natal-plum (*Carissa grandiflora*) in upright style is 7 years old. It has been in training 3 years. Trunk will thicken with age.

Another Natal-plum, 6 years in training, 23 inches high. Left unpruned for photo, then pinched to shape top and branches.

Gregg R. Wadleigh

LETTER FROM THE

BROOKLYN BOTANIC GARDEN

Bonsai has had a special fascination for Americans in the last several decades, the interest having been spurred initially by GI's returning from Japan after the Second World War. What a mystery it was for a potential monarch of the forest to be grown indefinitely in a small container, an attractive miniature in all its parts. Hadn't we grown up to believe that bigger was always better? How could the tree live—and be a creation of art at the same time? The appearance of two Brooklyn Botanic Garden Handbooks, *Dwarfed Potted Trees* (1953) and *Bonsai: Special Techniques* (1966) helped unravel the mystery for many westerners.

In the early years of "American" bonsai—and even now, plants were lost for needless reasons. Because bonsai trees attracted the fancy (often passing) of a wider public, they were treated as inanimate art objects by some, not as living natural things that had to be nurtured daily. Failure resulted and mystery became enigma. But not to all. The pioneer short courses in bonsai conducted at the Garden in the 1950's by Dr. George Avery (now Director Emeritus) and Bonsai Man Frank Okamura were practical guides for those who wanted to get off on the right track. Such popular courses are still given and people often fly in from different parts of the country to participate.

There was another, more subtle reason for many people's lack of success with bonsai. Early practitioners on this side of the Pacific were often excellent students of the Japanese. This was fine so far as technique was concerned, not necessarily so fine as to the plants chosen. Bonsai in Japan evolved slowly over many centuries and the plants selected there were the best possible ones—for Japanese growing conditions and climate. The art did not have its origins in hot, dry, sometimes poorly lit apartments—the only condition that many Americans can provide for plants in the late twentieth century. The pines and other northland trees so loved by the Japanese usually withered in western homes.

Americans were great copiers, but could they innovate? Was it possible to adapt bonsai techniques to plants that are better suited for indoors? A few people such as Constance Derderian, Ernesta Ballard, Sigmund Dreilinger, Frank Okamura and the late George Hull began to quietly, sometimes casually, experiment with house plants. Indoor bonsai is still a new field and some traditional students may be displeased with any adaptation. There are no 100-year-old classics of indoor bonsai sculptured by time and succeeding generations of grand masters. Still, it makes uncommon sense to create new treasures with plants that will live and thrive in the home, where they can be appreciated year round.

Let us take a moment to thank Guest Editor Constance Derderian and her twenty Contributors for this pioneering effort. Mrs. Derderian, who took the first bonsai course B.B.G. ever offered, has become one of the country's leading proponents of subtropical bonsai, and her enthusiasm is contagious. Let this be a kind invitation to wander through these pages and discover a new dimension to an old art.

A final thought. People sometimes lament to Frank Okamura that they don't have enough patience for bonsai. Mr. Okamura quietly replies: "Patience is what you need when you don't like what you're doing." And that is one of the many spirits of bonsai.

Sincerely,

Frederick Mc Gowrty

Editor

3

INTRODUCTION

Constance T. Derderian

THE INTEREST in house plants has grown to such a degree that now people who might never have tried indoor horticulture are becoming experts. For these people as well as the traditional bonsai enthusiast, indoor bonsai is a challenging new field to conquer. The pleasure of trying to grow different plants and the wonder of succeeding is ever new and possible for the person who seriously sets upon this pursuit.

Bonsai at first look may not be for everyone. For there is always someone who simply does not have the situation for growing anything in the home, let alone bonsai. Yet this person can create a suitable environment, as might be provided by an artificial light unit. Each potential growing situation should be assessed for light, moisture and temperature, and adjustments made as necessary. The translation of information enabling one to adjust the situation has to be done by each person for himself because growing conditions in the home vary tremendously.

The literal translation of the word bonsai is to plant in a shallow pot. Over the centuries it has come to mean tree in a shallow container—a *very refined* version of a tree. Every tree in a shallow container, however, is not a bonsai. It is a

Gregg R. Wadleigh

Varied selection of mame bonsai aged 2 months to 4 years in training, arranged on 18 inch stand.

question of merit, with appropriate form attained by pruning, wiring and other techniques, and it is here that the novice becomes confused. With practice one learns whether a tree in a container is a good bonsai. The pursuit of this kind of knowledge can be one of the more exciting adventures in learning about plants.

Growing bonsai indoors is a relatively new field. Subtropical plants have been grown as house plants for years but not in the Japanese manner. More recently these subtropicals have been grown as outdoor bonsai in Florida and California, but only now are they coming into homes all over the country. The growers of tra-ditional bonsai who have had to exchange houses for apartments, retirees who have moved from the North to the Sunbelt and house plant growers everywhere with increasingly refined tastes have created a need for information on growing bonsai indoors using subtropical plant materials.

We have asked people in several parts of the country to tell us how they grow their bonsai indoors and what they grow. Some are professionals, others are accomplished amateurs; all are innovators. Let them share their experiences with you so you can be off to a fine start in one of horticulture's most fascinating new ventures.

Living with plants

BONSAI IN THE HOUSE
Ernesta and Fred Ballard

FOR more than twenty years we have lived with plants. We share our bedroom with a 6-foot areca palm; our living room with a gardenia, two figs, another large palm and a number of smaller species; our hall with a 6-foot fig, a 5-foot schefflera, more palms, a podocarpus, a climbing fern, a tree fern, a Chinese-evergreen, an ancient aspidistra, and assorted others; our dining room with a medinilla, a weeping podocarpus, still another large palm, an araucaria tree, and again a miscellany of smaller plants, often changed to suit the season.

There are plants in the study, kitchen, cellar and offices. Many of them have lived with us for ten or fifteen years. So when we speak of indoor bonsai we mean bonsai living in spaces where people can live comfortably twenty-four hours a day. We exclude all special environments such as glass-roofed sunporches, recessed windows with interior glass and window greenhouses.

As far as horticultural literature is concerned, there is no such topic as indoor bonsai. Those who want to grow dwarf potted trees indoors year-round have to read standard bonsai texts for aesthetics and training techniques and indoor gardening texts for horticultural information and practice. Even after this preparation there is much trial and error, with the results dependent on the particular conditions in which the plants must live in the house.

Climate Differences

The reason why there is no comprehensive treatise on indoor bonsai is that the word "indoors" covers a vast range of conditions—from an unheated bungalow in southern Florida to a 70° apartment in Boston. At the southern end of this range it is possible to grow a tremendous variety of plants indoors. At the northern end the indoor conditions are tolerable for relatively few species. When friends tell you what

Fig. 1. Jade plant *(Crassula argentea)*.

E.B. Gilchrist, Jr.

However, when it comes to predictions for individual species, there are no guidelines but experience. You cannot determine in advance whether the charming shrub seen growing in the Everglades can be acclimated to a New England dwelling, although it is a reasonably good bet that if the plant does not appear in any of the more complete texts on house plants, it has been tested and found wanting.

The reasons why some species survive moving into the house better than others are interesting. If you want to learn more about them, visit a good horticultural library and consult *Plant Geography Upon a Physiological Basis* by A. F. W. Schimper, published in 1903. It is still the best statement of why a five-needle pine or a trident maple from the cool-temperate areas of the world won't grow successfully on a windowsill. Dr. Schimper tells us that the life of a plant is made up of thousands of separate actions, each performed within its own range of temperatures, and that the critical temperatures for different functions differ by only a degree or so in "equable climates," but by many degrees in colder regions. This explains in a general way why tropical plants can be grown at uniformly high temperatures, while plants of the North, where there are sharp temperature differences between summer and winter and even between day and night, need alternate highs and lows, with the lows often below freezing. It also explains why the low temperature is critical in indoor gardening.

they grow in their houses, don't assume that you can do the same unless there are comparable conditions for the vital factors of plant growth—light, temperature (especially the low temperature at night) and atmospheric humidity.

When a bonsai fancier follows his natural instincts by collecting a specimen in the wild, putting it in a pot and bringing it into his house, he is, for practical purposes, moving it from one climate to another. The same is true when he buys a plant grown in a sunny greenhouse and settles it on his windowsill. Indeed, any plant indoors has been moved to an unnatural climate.

The effect that such a change in climate will have on a plant is roughly proportional to the difference between its native habitat and the artificial environment to which it has been transported. Since the climate indoors generally resembles the tropics and subtropics, at least as to temperature, plants from these regions will usually perform better in the house than natives of the northern temperate zone.

Plants to Grow

What does this mean in practice? For long-term success with bonsai in the house you cannot use the traditional favorites of the Japanese, such as the

E. B. Gilchrist, Jr.

Fig. 2. *Araucaria bidwillii.*

pines, maples, spruces and beeches, that are native to the colder reaches. Choose a plant that will grow indoors, whether or not that plant appears in the Japanese bonsai texts. For example, one of the toughest of all house plants, capable of enduring high heat, low humidity and poor illumination, is the jade plant (*Crassula argentea*). For growing in the house, it can scarcely be beaten, but can you make a bonsai out of it?

The answer depends on your concept of bonsai. If all that will satisfy you are faithful reproductions of the plants displayed at bonsai exhibitions in Japan, you will not take kindly to a jade plant. But, on the other hand, if your idea of bonsai encompasses any woody plant trained to a decorative shape and planted in a complementary container, you may find that the jade plant has much to offer. Figure 1 shows what can be done with it.

Once you have accepted the notion of a jade plant, so manifestly a native of South Africa, planted in a container so man-

ifestly made in Japan, you are on your way to developing house plant bonsai. Other articles in this Handbook tell about particular species that have been used successfully, any of which might be suitable for your conditions. However, before we turn you over to our fellow contributors, there are a few more points that should be made:

Bonsai can be grown in more ornamental containers indoors than out. Figure 2 shows our Australian araucaria, *A. bidwillii*, in a blue and white porcelain pot from China. The free form shape, precarious balance, and fragile container would be out of place in a garden, but they make a striking decoration in the dining room.

It is often easier to treat tropical plants as large bonsai rather than small ones, because the leaves tend to be big and the internodal spaces long. The araucaria in figure 2 stands nearly 5 feet tall. We also have an American wonder lemon (*Citrus limon* 'Ponderosa') at least 6 feet in height and 4 feet across—too big for many houses, but very satisfactory if there is the space.

At the other end of the scale, we are just learning how to grow diminutive tropical bonsai under artificial illumination. For example, the normal distance from the base of the petiole to the end of the leaf in a schefflera (*Brassaia actinophylla*) grown indoors is about 30 inches. But we have one growing in a kitchen light unit for which the corresponding dimension is 3 inches, a tenfold reduction in scale. The trick is to grow the plant in a very small container no more than 6 inches below the lights, to pinch the growing tip frequently, and to cut off any leaf that exceeds the desired size. The same general treatment has succeeded with various ficus, pittosporum (*P. tobira*), finger-aralia (*Dizygotheca elegantissima*) and indoor-oak (*Nicodemia diversifolia*). We expect it will work with many other plants from mild climates.

One of the challenges of working with tropical material is to capture the feel of the trees in their native habitat, which is often quite different from the feel of temperate-zone dwellers. Figure 3 shows a huge ficus (note the man in the foreground) with the surface root formation that many members of this genus have. There is also a strangler fig (*Ficus aurea*) in our collection displaying the beginning of a similar formation. The olive trees of the Mediterranean countries are another example of a distinctive habit of growth, and figure 4 shows a specimen of *Olea europaea* in which we have tried to capture this habit.

If you are set on reproducing traditional Japanese bonsai indoors, try junipers and cypresses: San Jose juniper (*Juniperus chinensis* 'San Jose') and Monterey and Arizona cypresses (*Cupressus macrocarpa*, *C. arizonica*) have done well for us. Also, if you can lower the night temperature below 65°, you may have success with pomegranates, such as the specimen shown in figure 5. From the warmer regions of Japan and other parts of Asia there are plants such as the sago-palm (*Cycas revoluta*) and yew podocarpus (*P. macrophyllus*), which the Japanese grow as bonsai. These are adaptable indoors, too. Figure 6 shows an example of the former.

Since the growing conditions in the particular house are important, it may be helpful to note that in our own home the night temperatures in winter normally drop below 65°, sometimes as low as 62°. Except when the sun is on the plants, the day temperatures rarely exceed 68°. The house is noticeably cooler than most apartments, and consquently more humid, even though there is no humidifier. This enables us to grow the sometimes difficult gardenia (*G. jasminoides*). The coolness and humidity help prevent the premature dropping of flower buds, which is one of the common problems in growing this plant indoors. All the bonsai pictured in this article have

Fig. 3. Spotted fig (*Ficus virens*), of great size and age, photographed in China at the turn of the century by noted plant explorer E. H. Wilson.

E. B. Gilchrist, Jr.

Fig. 4. Olive *(Olea europaea)*.

Vinciguerra

Fig. 5. Pomegranate
(Punica granatum).

E. B. Gilchrist, Jr.

Fig. 6. Sago-palm
(*Cycas revoluta*).

spent at least one winter in our house.
Most of them spend every winter there.

Adaptation of Bonsai

Some years ago the authors collaborated
on a book called *The Art of Training
Plants*.* It described a wide variety of
decorative plants and showed how all of
them reflected to a considerable degree
the philosophy and technique of bonsai.
Our view today is essentially the
same—bonsai principles should not be
confined to the reproduction of classic
styles, but should be used to create new
forms in tune with contemporary American concepts of art. Particularly is this
true indoors, where plants should be
elegant and ornamental.

No one should undertake to shape trees

ed.—now available as a soft cover edition in
the Everyday Handbook Series, published by
Barnes & Noble, a division of Harper & Row.

and woody plants, indoors or out, without a thorough grounding in traditional
bonsai. However, we hope that readers of
this Handbook will go further and produce American styles as typical of our
culture as the conventional styles are typical of the Japanese way of living. The
noted Japanese grower, Kyuzo Murata,
in PLANTS & GARDENS (Vol. 31, No.
4), stated that the final goal of creating
bonsai is to create a feeling of *Wabi* (a
feeling of quiet, dignified simplicity associated with a place) or *Sabi* (a feeling of
simplicity and quietness associated with
something that is old and used over and
over again). The feeling of *Wabi* or *Sabi*,
he said, is something almost stoic which
eventually leads to Zen Buddhism. We
look forward to the day when American
growers will find in their creations attri-
butes that mean as much to us as *Wabi*
and *Sabi* mean to Mr. Murata. This
development may well begin with bonsai
in the house.

Signs of growth are apparent every day . . .

INDOOR BONSAI ARE DIFFERENT

Warren P. Cooper and Jerald P. Stowell

THE real secret of successful indoor bonsai is the proper selection of plant material— plants that take to the apartment environment. Good bonsai can be developed from semi-hardy trees and shrubs. Many woody tropicals, although they tend to look more herbaceous in young growth, are also fine choices. There is a wide range of possibilities, and each grower should want to select plants that will grow best in his home. For a list of potentially good indoor bonsai, see page 50.

Growth Rate and Pruning

Indoor bonsai, being largely tropical or semi-tropical, mature at least as fast as those from the temperate zones, and their appearance changes rapidly. Signs of growth are apparent every day, and the pleasurable treatments of pinching and pruning are frequently called for.

The techniques of pruning, root pruning and potting indoor bonsai are essentially the same as for spruces, pines, maples and other more traditional material. Growth takes place throughout the whole year, though it proceeds at a very much slower rate in autumn and early winter. A tropical tree gives the appearance of maturity in eight to ten years, whereas a tree or shrub from the temperate zone might require twice as long to attain the same venerable patina.

Pruning is important for any bonsai, but indoor trees tend to greater legginess and lose their shape more quickly than outdoor trees. Without constant attention to form, the intricate branching pattern that signals a beautiful bonsai will not develop. Trimming new growth is a continuing practice. Deciduous plants and broad-leaved evergreens have their new growth shortened. Conifers have their new shoots pinched back to leave only four or five clusters of needles at the base.

Watering and Fertilizing

Beware of the old wives' tale that bonsai are dwarfed by withholding water. The dwarf quality is due to pruning and container restriction. The trees should never be kept soggy, but neither should they be allowed to dry out completely, since this will cause damage to the root system.

Bonsai growers have different methods of watering. We feel that the trees should be watered thoroughly from the top, and the leaves should be frequently moistened. A florist's syringe is a good instrument to use in-between if each bonsai has been given a good watering. The spray, directed into the foliage, is especially beneficial to the plant in removing dust and normal city soot. One of the best places to water and syringe the plants is in the bathtub. Here you have no worry about watering tables, chairs and rugs along with the trees.

Proper fertilizing means good foliage color, well-formed flowers, an intricate branching system—in general a healthy, beautiful bonsai. The easiest complete fertilizer to use is one of the water-soluble products containing trace elements. These are made by several manufacturers and are available from any garden center. They should not be used full strength, however. It is best to dilute them by half. (See page 17 for more information.)

Indoor trees are fertilized during two seasons to keep them in good condition. A weak solution is applied once a week for three weeks in February to provide for forthcoming healthy growth. Too strong a solution when there is very little sun in winter will produce scraggly growth. However, if your indoor plant is one that goes dormant in the winter, it should not be fertilized until the new shoots appear in spring. Summer fertilizing is similar to outdoor care.

Criteria for indoors or out . . .

WHAT MAKES A GOOD BONSAI?

Mary P. Case

1. The container is of a style, shape and color to complement the style of the tree. Both are in harmony.

2. The surface roots, if any, make a gentle pattern radiating from the base of the trunk. No roots are crossed one over the other, nor are any exposed in an extreme or unnatural manner unless this is in keeping with the style of the tree.

3. The trunk is positioned in the container in an aesthetically satisfying spot for its particular style. Approximately the first (bottom) third of the trunk is clearly visible, and the second third is partially visible. The trunk tapers from the earth to the tip of the tree. There are no abrupt or artificial changes.

4. The main branches are gracefully arranged left, right and rear of the trunk. The distance between them is of equal or nearly equal proportion on all parts of the tree. None crosses another.

5. The twigs which grow from the branches make delicate and precise patterns, all of about the same length. If there are training wires, they are applied neatly to both branch and twig. The wires are of a dull color so they do not disturb the overall effect more than necessary. A 'finished' bonsai has no wires.

6. Leaves, flowers and fruits are all in good proportion for the size of the tree.

7. If the tree is grown partly for its ornamental fruits, they are arranged in a balanced fashion upon the branches. Should they be a little large, a number are removed to achieve a more natural presentation.

8. There is no evidence of stubs left from pruning or marks from wires, weights, or other props used in training.

Adapted from *Tropical Bonsai*, American Bonsai Society, 1967.

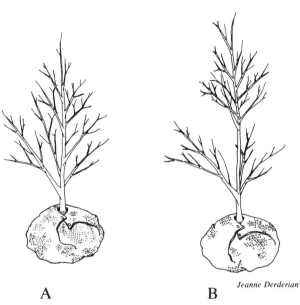

Jeanne Derderian

A   B

Two trees from nursery. A shows more potential than B because of the more numerous, better spaced branches.

12

Preliminary pruning and possible subsequent training of tree A.

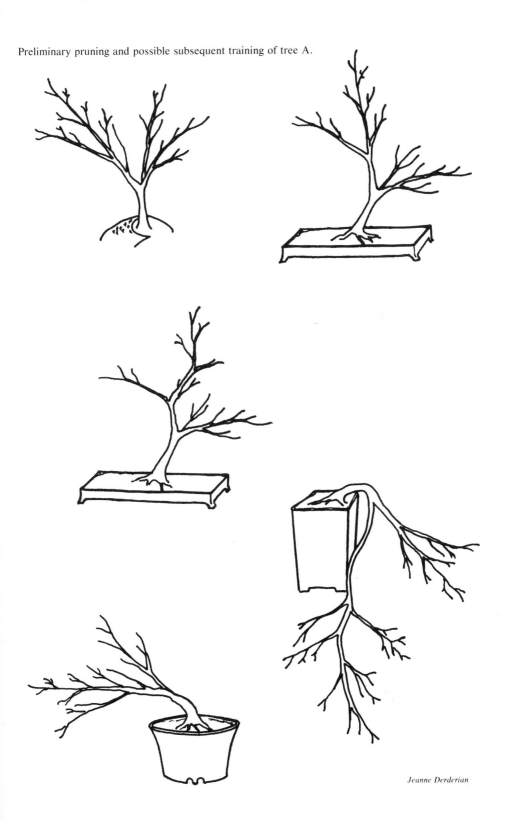

Jeanne Derderian

A BONSAI REFRESHER

Constance T. Derderian

THE JOY OF BONSAI is in the doing. To buy one is a short cut, but you will lose by this method. To really understand bonsai you must create one yourself. Read, look at examples—real or pictured, and if at all possible, take a few lessons.

Begin with a rugged, amateur-resistant plant such as the dwarf powder-puff (*Calliandra emarginata*), Confederate-jasmine (*Trachelospermum jasminoides*), brush-cherry (*Syzygium paniculatum*; often sold as *Eugenia myrtifolia*), or a small-leaved ficus. One or more of these subtropical plants can be found in almost any house-plant nursery or florist shop.

Containers and Soils

Choose the container, keeping in mind the size of the plant and the bonsai style you wish to develop. (See page 29.) If an upright style is desired, almost any bonsai container of the low rectangular, oval, round or square shapes will do. Deeper containers are used for the semi-cascade or cascade styles. Do not worry about making a mistake for plants can always be repotted when you learn more. If you prefer, selecting a container can be left until after the bonsai has been shaped and styled in an ordinary clay or plastic pot. Bonsai containers may take a bit of hunting, but an increasing number of local garden centers, gift shops and even department stores are carrying them.

For the indoor gardener who does not have access to soil or compost, the mysteries of soil are best dealt with by using a commercial all-purpose potting mix and adding sand (approximately 1/6 to 1/3 by volume because such a mix already has some sand in it). An easy-to-find substitute for sand is bird gravel. Whatever is used, free draining soil is important.

If you prefer to learn to mix your own, start with the indoor gardener's basic 1/3 loam, 1/3 peat moss, 1/3 sand. Packaged loam is pasteurized, but loam from the garden is not. Good rule to remember: if you dig it, cook it! This is done by baking the loam in a preheated oven at 200° F for half an hour.

After experimenting with the proportions, you will settle on the mix that is best for you. Regardless of the combination, it is best to put each component into a fine sieve to remove the fine powder particles and insure good drainage. The part that goes through the sieve is thrown away, and the part remaining *above* is used. Bonsai soil is used dry so that it will move down through the roots easily when potting up.

Tools and Pruning

The tools needed for bonsai are few: sharp scissors, good pruning shears, a wire cutter and one unusual implement for westerners—a chopstick (even a knitting needle will do). There are excellent tools made especially for the bonsai grower. They make the work neater as well as easier but can be acquired as your interest and knowledge grow.

Start shaping the tree in the chosen style by removing unnecessary branches and shortening the remaining ones if needed. Wiring, if any is necessary, should be applied at this time—doing it after the plant is in the container wiggles the tree and can damage the roots that are left. For a discussion of wiring see page 19. When the general shape is achieved, the plant is ready for potting up. The fine pruning, pinching and adjusting of the branches, is done after the plant is in the container.

Potting and Placement

When the preliminary shaping is done, take the plant, (whose soil should be on the dry side for this operation) and with a chopstick reduce the root ball by removing soil and cutting away the exposed roots. Don't disturb the soil immediately around and below the trunk.

14

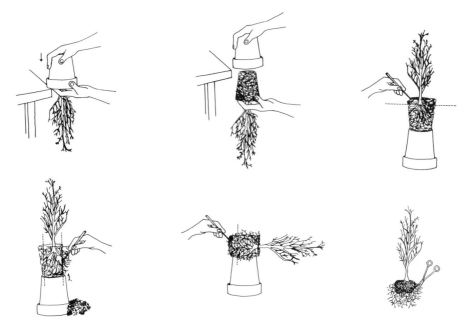

Jeanne Derderian

Remove plant from pot; using chopstick or similar tool, tease soil away from roots, leaving a central ball of soil; trim roots—especially older, woody ones—leaving young and fibrous roots in center; repot.

With the vigorous subtropical material used for indoor bonsai, up to two-thirds of the roots can be cut away. A beginner should err on the side of safety and do less rather than more. At this point, the plant is ready to put into the container.

If the first container is too large, don't worry about it because the plant will grow well even if it is out of scale. Later, when potting techniques become familiar, the bonsai can be potted down—that is, put into a smaller container. Placement in the container should be slightly off center and slightly to the rear of the intended viewing side. Sometimes a heavy root will not allow correct placement. Do the best you can and cut the heavy root back at the next potting.

For subtropicals, repotting depends on the growth of the plant. Some grow very slowly in a small container and do not need a yearly root pruning. When in doubt, however, do it once a year in the spring. After potting, the bonsai is set in a basin with water up to the rim of the container until the soil is saturated. It will not need water again for a day or two. From then on I always water from the top.

A Ground Cover

Cover the surface of the soil so that it will not wash away. Moss, fine pebbles and finely ground bark are favored ground covers. Baby's-tears (*Helxine*) and other tiny-leaved creepers can be used if the container is large enough so that the creeper does not deplete the soil of nutrients or destroy the proportions.

Moss is the best cover for any bonsai. Experiment with different kinds growing in your area. If you are an apartment dweller, obtain some from a greenhouse, where it is often found growing freely on the benches. Although moss thrives under moist conditions, some bonsai plants grow best on the dry side. Misting the moss surface lightly and frequently is the solution.

15

Subtropical materials often have an innate grace that is well suited to decorative containers.

Peter Chvany

Watering and Fertilizing

It may take five years to learn how to water some bonsai precisely, but don't let this discourage you. Avoid extremes. Never let the plant dry out completely, but don't keep it constantly wet, either. Watering once a day is usually enough, depending on the light and the temperature. If a certain plant needs to be grown on the dry side, a small amount of water daily or a liberal watering every other day is a technique to use. Try each way to see which is best for the plant. Occasionally a bonsai can be watered by soaking it in a basin of water, but I do not recommend doing this regularly.

Because bonsai soil is free draining and frequently watered, the nutrients are rather quickly drained out. Fertilizing regularly will help to keep the bonsai healthy, and a small amount of soluble fertilizer weekly is better than a large dose monthly. The new grower should probably begin with a soluble 5-10-5, a balanced fertilizer having twice as much

Nursery stock of dwarf powder-puff (*Calliandra emarginata*) temporarily overpotted to allow maximum growth to thicken trunk and branches.

16

phosphorus ("10") as nitrogen (the first "5") and potassium (the second "5"). Avoid fertilizers with a high proportion of nitrogen because growth will be too lush and will defeat the bonsai purpose.

Whatever soluble fertilizer is chosen, use it at half the strength recommended on the package and then dilute it even further if it is to be used more frequently than specified in the directions.

Example:
Directions say 1 tsp. to a quart of water, once every two weeks.
For bonsai use—1/2 tsp. to a quart of water, once every two weeks or—1/4 tsp. to a quart of water, once a week or ten days.

Pests

Sooner or later one learns about the common plant pests such as mealy bug, scale, white fly, and, worst of all, spider mites. To help prevent them, keep the plant healthy and the air circulating. Wash the foliage, including the underside, with the sink spray about once a week. Learn to recognize the pests for they can then be dealt with before doing too much harm. A simple method is to dunk the entire plant in lukewarm, soapy (not detergent) water and then rinse, or brush the affected areas with rubbing alcohol and finish with a clean water rinse. Out of necessity I have brushed the entire plant with alcohol with no adverse effects. If more than this is needed, use an appropriate house-plant insecticide. Take special precautions because any spraying in the home, even with a carefully aimed aerosol, has its risks.

Use a large box or plastic bag to contain the plant and restrict the spray or, using rubber gloves, brush a dilute solution of insecticide over the plant. Regardless of method, protect the soil with plastic from any drippings.

"The longest journey begins with a single step," is a quote from the Chinese. Bonsai is an exacting art with living plants and you may be discouraged at times. However, take the first step. If your initial bonsai does not survive (and it may very well not) apply what you have learned to the second. Read a bit more or take another lesson. Soon there will be more success than failure and then your journey is confidently under way.

Stacy Holmes

Interior of window greenhouse, ideal for maximum sun with winter protection for indoor bonsai.

WIRING

Constance T. Derderian

SOMETIMES it is possible to shape a bonsai exclusively by pruning and trimming, but in many cases wiring is necessary to change the angle or direction of a trunk, branch or twig. Major wiring is best and most easily done just before the plant is potted up. Minor wiring can be done at other times, preferably when the plant is actively growing, but care should be taken not to disturb the roots in the container while doing it.

Use copper wire because this type holds its position best. It is available from hardware stores in different gauges, nos. 10 to 22 being most appropriate. The gauge of the wire depends on the diameter of the trunk or limb to be treated. Occasionally a heavier-than-usual wire is necessary because a particular branch is very resilient; use two smaller wires if you do not have one heavy enough. Sometimes it is wise to wrap the wire with florist tape to protect the bark.

Whatever is done, take care not to wind the wood too tightly or the pressure will scar the bark. The duration of wiring depends on the vigor of growth at the time. Overall growth rate of the particular species and size of the branch are also factors. Sometimes three to six weeks are enough for indoor bonsai, occasionally a longer time is needed.

Subtropical plants are in general much faster growing than ones from the temperate parts of the world, so frequent inspection of the wire is wise. It is not uncommon for branches to be wired a second time. Make sure to unwind the first set of wires with care. Rewiring, if necessary, is done immediately.

Here is how different parts of the tree are treated:

Trunk—begin at the base by inserting the wire at least 1 1/2 inches to 2 inches into the soil and coil upward spacing evenly. Avoid passing the wire too closely to where the branches meet the trunk.

Branches—begin by anchoring wire firmly by passing it at least one full spiral around the trunk or, if two branches are to be wired, use one piece of wire winding the middle portion around the trunk between the two branches and continuing on out toward the end of the branch.

Twigs—begin by securing wire by spiraling it twice around the branch so it won't wobble when bending the twig.

If the coil is too far apart it will not hold its position. If it is too close together, it will injure the bark in the bending and look ugly.

When branch wire is added where there is already trunk wire, the branch wire should closely parallel the larger wire so it is neat and doesn't disturb the eye. The same applies to twig wires.

WIRING TECHNIQUES

"Never be in a hurry. . . . It is the hands which must do the learning, slowly and repeatedly until they can think for you." —Yashiroda

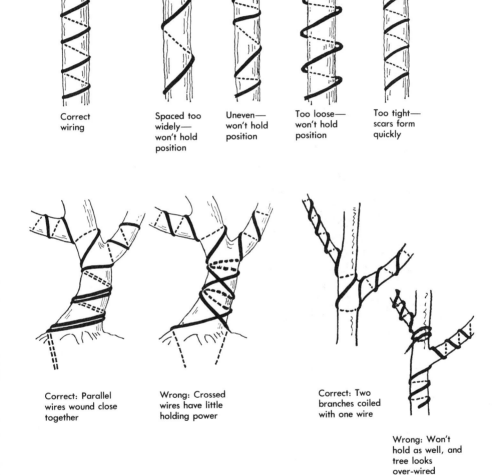

THIS

NOT THESE

Correct wiring

Spaced too widely— won't hold position

Uneven— won't hold position

Too loose— won't hold position

Too tight— scars form quickly

Correct: Parallel wires wound close together

Wrong: Crossed wires have little holding power

Correct: Two branches coiled with one wire

Wrong: Won't hold as well, and tree looks over-wired

Begin wiring at bottom of tree and work upward. If trunk is to be wired, anchor wire ends by pushing down through root ball to a bottom corner of container. Avoid sheating a tree in wire; good wiring practices give best results with least wiring.

All drawings adapted from Toshio Kawamoto and Joseph Y. Kurihara, Bonsai-Saikei.

SHAPING A TREE WITH WIRE

*"Wiring has two purposes: to help the tree attain its ideal form,
and to correct overlapping branches so that all can receive the sun
and evening dew." —Saburo Kato*

Branches growing upward can be trained to slope downward or outward, suggesting the form of an aged tree.

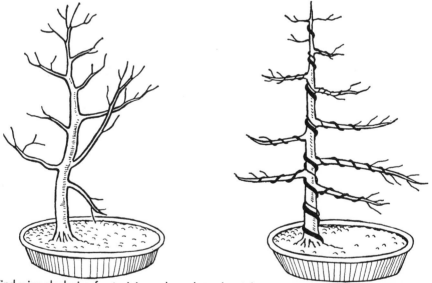

Wind wire clockwise for training a branch to the right, counterclockwise for training it to the left. Wire should be of a size just stiff enough to hold newly bent branch in position.

Drawings adapted from Toshio Kawamoto and Joseph Y. Kurihara, Bonsai-Sakei.

20

Preparation of Container

Hardware cloth or plastic screen is used to cover drainage holes. Gravel is then spread on the bottom of the pot for drainage. (The larger the pot, the larger the size of gravel you should use.) If the plant is big or top heavy and needs support while the roots get established, copper wire is inserted through the bottom of the container before potting, the plant is inserted, and the ends of the wire are bent up and around the root ball. (See diagram for anchoring wire if the pot has only one hole.) For added security for top-heavy plants anchor the wire and bring the free end up through the root ball. Use this to wire the plant trunk and branches. The ends of the wire are hidden by the top of the soil mix. Remove the wire after the plant has rooted well. —*Edmond O. Moulin*.

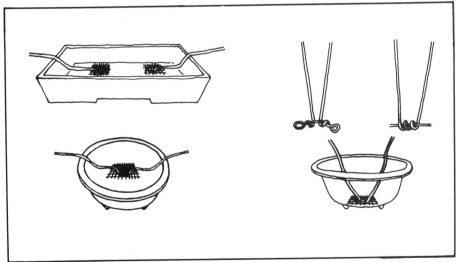

Jeanne Derderian

If the pot has only one drainage hole, twist wire like a candy wrapper or wrap it around a finishing nail so it will straddle the hole and be anchored to the underside of the pot.

A Window Case For Bonsai

A recessed window becomes an indoor bonsai display and growing area. These shelves, or a similar design, can be adapted to other types of windows, sliding glass doors or floor-to-ceiling glass panels.

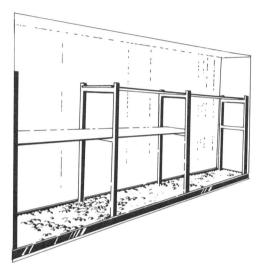

Left: Schematic drawing of finished shelf.

Below: Glass shelves in redwood frame for bonsai culture are removable for window cleaning. Installation of sliding glass panels adapts window for temperate zone bonsai that need winter chilling treatment

Drawings by Ivy Mitchell

Hutchins Photography

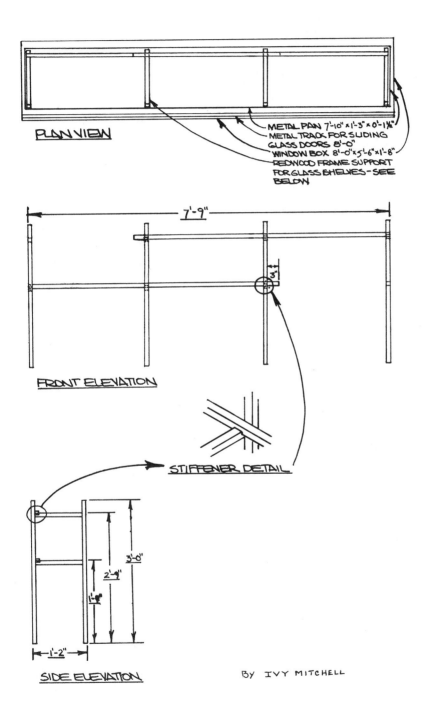

PLAN VIEW

METAL PAN 7'-10" x 1'-3" x 0'-1½"
METAL TRACK FOR SLIDING
GLASS DOORS 8'-0"
WINDOW BOX 8'-0" x 5'-6" x 1'-8"
REDWOOD FRAME SUPPORT
FOR GLASS SHELVES — SEE
BELOW

7'-9"

3"

FRONT ELEVATION

STIFFENER DETAIL

3'-0"

2'-4"

1'-2"

SIDE ELEVATION

BY IVY MITCHELL

If you can grow house plants,
you can grow indoor bonsai

CARE—PRELIMINARY REQUIREMENTS

Edmond O. Moulin

INDOOR PLANTS for bonsai? Why not? It makes excellent sense to experiment with them. By adapting the traditional pruning and potting techniques practiced by the Japanese it is possible to bring a refreshing innovation to much material previously untried as bonsai.

Light

Let's talk about some of the preliminary and necessary requirements for growing indoor bonsai successfully. All plants require light and bonsai are no exception. Those with flowers and fruits often need more light than most. Plants grown indoors never receive quite as much light as their counterparts outdoors, so their placement within the home becomes all the more important. If at all possible, choose an unobstructed east, west or south window. The last site is best in winter, especially for plants with the greatest light requirements.

There is no need to despair if your natural light indoors is less than adequate. A wide variety of modestly priced units are now available, as well as automatic timers. Vita-Lite, Agro-lite or the cool white fluorescent tubes combined with incandescent bulbs may be used on indoor bonsai with excellent results. The practice is to provide artificial light for about sixteen hours a day at a distance of 4 to 12 inches above the plant material. More light can be provided by vertical banks of fluorescent lamps.

Temperature and Humidity

Temperature is another important cultural factor to consider. Most people are comfortable with a house temperature of a constant 68°—72° F day and night. Plants generally perform better if the temperature at night is ten or fifteen degrees cooler than in the day. Fortunately, however, both people and plants are moderately adaptable creatures. First, consider lowering the thermostat a few degrees at night. It's a good conservation practice these days anyway, heating bills will be less, and the plants will grow better.

Another point to remember is that even our modern, centrally heated homes have microclimates of sorts, and these may be put to work for indoor bonsai. Thermostats are usually set at eye level, but the temperature near the floor is lower. In a well-ventilated house the temperature can vary as much as ten degrees for every 3 feet of height. An additional way of providing a cooler location for indoor bonsai is to place them between the window and a pair of heavy drapes. At night when the drapes are closed, the lower temperature will benefit the plants.

The worst enemy of indoor bonsai is dryness, for our contemporary abodes are as arid as the Sahara. The higher the temperature is, the lower the relative amount of moisture in the air will be. There are various corrective measures to be sure, including installation of a humidifier, revival of the Victorian technique of grouping plants, misting of foliage (though this has but brief benefit) and the placement of pots on moist gravel. Some innovative gardeners have even experimented with growing indoor bonsai in modified terrariums, enclosed but away from the direct rays of the sun.

In Summer

All plants benefit from being outside during the summer if space is available in areas protected from winds. Plants can safely be placed outside after the last predicted frost date for your area and, better yet, when the night temperature does not fall below 55° F.

24

David Fukumoto

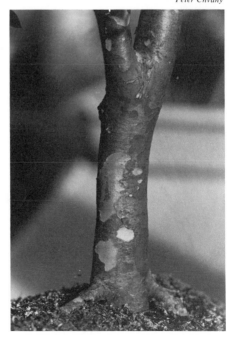

Bark and roots of cajeput-tree
(*Melaleuca quinquenervia*) develop
character with age.

an open window having good light. There should be no strong drafts of either heated or cooled air. Rotate plants every other day—as should be done during any season of year. If the only window is on the south side of the building, keep the plants back several feet for a couple of weeks to prevent burning by the hot sun. Gradually the plants can be moved closer to the window but never put on the windowsill because of the danger of a pot falling. Plan to syringe the foliage even more than in winter because of soot and dust.

Do not be dissuaded from growing indoor bonsai because a few extra steps are involved in their care. This is an exciting new way of growing plants and you can put your imagination to work in a beautifully creative fashion. Remember, if you can grow house plants, you can grow indoor bonsai.

As with all plants grown indoors, bonsai should not be set immediately in full sun outdoors. Gradually acclimate the plant by moving it from a shadier location outdoors to filtered sun and then to full sun (for those species which benefit from full sun). The two-to-three week period of acclimation allows the cutin (wax layer) of the leaves to develop in the presence of the ultra-violet rays of the sun.

Of course, watering during the summer will be much more frequent and a critical factor to regard. Plants should be moved indoors in late summer or early autumn *before* the night temperature drops below 55° F. The plant should have at least a few weeks of adjustment before the heat is turned on. The usual practice of retrieving a plant on the night a frost is predicted and then plunking it in the heated home often causes problems and frequently results in the death of the plant.

If you live in a high-rise apartment with no balcony or fire escape for bonsai summer vacations, try to place the plants near

Peter Chvany

Jaboticaba (*Myrciaria cauliflora*) has handsome, multicolor exfoliating bark.

Techniques for keeping
indoor bonsai healthy

PRUNING CAN MAKE
THE DIFFERENCE

John Yoshio Naka

To GROW an indoor bonsai takes skill and care beyond selecting a suitable plant. The reasons why the more traditional bonsai plants die after being kept indoors for any length of time is that lacking are such natural elements as necessary light, air circulation, humidity and, of course, rain and dew.

However, once a suitable plant has been selected that will thrive under most indoor conditions, satisfactory results can be achieved, especially with pruning and trimming. If not properly pruned, the tree will lose compactness, which is very important for a bonsai. Keeping it too bushy will cause it to lose its leaves and some of the small center branches. If the tree becomes too weakened, it will be more susceptible to diseases and insects. More care and caution are needed to maintain an indoor bonsai in a healthy condition.

The following are guidelines on pruning and trimming to shape a bonsai and keep it healthy indoors.

This bonsai has reached a very bushy stage and none of the details such as the trunk, branches or a definite apex can be seen. Eventually the center of the tree will die out.

Prune and trim to expose the trunk and branches. Indicate a definite apex and create a triangular outline of the tree. This will keep the inside branches healthy and compact.

All drawings by J. Y. Naka

26

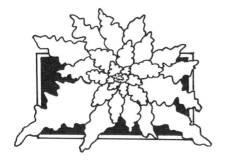

Prune all excess branches so they do not overlap any other branches when viewed from the top. Each branch should be placed in a different direction so it will receive light. This arrangement will also give the bonsai depth.

All sides of tree must be rotated to receive either the sunlight or artificial light. If kept in one position too long, the side receiving the light will get bushy and the opposite side will become weak and straggly.

If the plant is lopsided due to uneven light, the stronger side must be drastically pruned back to the same structure as the weaker side. The weaker side should be pruned, too, especially all the dead branches. Be sure to rotate the plant evenly after this.

Without regular pruning the tree will become top heavy, causing the interior branches to die back and, due to leggy growth, it will assume a bulky appearance.

The heavy top should be cut back drastically by removing the long and large branches, and leaving only the small and short ones. Prune back to original apex. Treat any large scars with sealing compound. The lowest branch should be the longest and the largest in diameter. Trim the small branches and cut back any dead ones.

Leave all fresh growth alone until the tree establishes strength.

Then shape it by trimming and wiring. If there is plenty of growth growing sideways, then any growth pointing downwards or upwards should be removed. If not they should all be wired and trained to go sideways to form a flat plane.

Strive for a natural form

BONSAI STYLES
Constance T. Derderian

THE REQUIREMENTS for good bonsai material common to all styles are a nicely tapering trunk, evenly spaced branches diminishing in thickness of limb from base to apex, compact growth and small leaves. Some kinds of plants can be used in more than one style. As with traditional bonsai, strive for a natural form. A good bonsai is one which imparts the feeling of nature in miniature.

The style of the bonsai is dependent upon the structure of the plant material. *Formal upright*, with its precise requirements, is perhaps the most difficult to achieve and maintain with subtropical plants and, to my way of thinking, not worth the effort required. *Informal upright* style is by far the outstanding form for indoor bonsai because the grower can work easily within its limits. A slightly curving trunk and three or more branches ("... one to the left, one to the right and one to the rear for depth") is easily found.

Slanting style is another favorite, espe-

cially of the novice, because he associates its look with bonsai. A leaning trunk and two lower branches are needed; sometimes only one will do, depth being provided by width in the lower branch and/or the shape of the top of the tree. *Semi-cascade* is an exaggerated slanting style. It may or may not have branches low on the trunk. The apex of the tree is on a level with, or slightly below, the rim of the container.

An unkind phrase which has grown out of bonsai study is, "When you don't know what to do with it—make a *cascade*." For the beginner it signifies an easy style; it isn't. A good cascade is a simple but deceiving form. It can have any number of branches, left, right and front (none to the back) and the apex of the tree extends beyond the bottom of the container. The one thing to avoid in a cascade is an upright trunk with an abrupt curve downward. The trunk should slant or be almost flat as it grows out of the container.

29

ILLUSTRATED GUIDE TO STYLES

Frank Okamura

Informal upright (Moyogi) style with
Shari branch (dry part within foliage).

Slanting style with gnarled Shari trunk
(aged dead wood).

Slanting style with Jin.

All drawings by Frank Okamura

Forest style. Illusion of distance by
sloping. Suggestion of mountains.

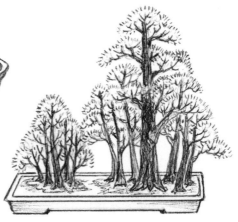

Two-group style. Suggestion of two
human families.

Clinging upright style with driftwood or
stone. Imagine a tree holding onto a
rock in a gorge.

Group slanting style.

Tornado Shari trunk with Jin, upright style. In Jin, exposed dead wood is above foliage and reaches toward heaven.

Cascade style with drooping-type tree.

Cascade style with pomegranate on rustic root stand. The trunk is partly decayed (Saba-mike).

MAME BONSAI

Doris W. Froning

Peter Chvany

Life size photo of false heather
(*Cuphea hyssopifolia*) begun
from cutting five years ago

A mame is usually any plant kept 6 inches or less tall and trained in bonsai style. It is a miniature even by bonsai standards. Mame, pronounce mah-may, means "little bean" in Japanese. Plants that can be grown as large bonsai can be grown in this miniature style provided they have naturally small foliage, short internodes and small flowers and fruit.

Attention to detail, including careful watering of the correspondingly small containers, is very important in mame bonsai. The shape of the plant can be the same as with larger bonsai but the grower is almost working with a shorthand version because there are rarely more than three branches. Some departure from traditional standards is acceptable because a graceful tree in a small pot is preferable to a stiff tree that follows all the rules. However, even the smallest mame must be well shaped. Putting a rooted cutting into a small pot and calling it a mame bonsai is wrong. Any plant needs some training to qualify as a bonsai.

Training a mame bonsai can be done with copper wire, using only the finer grades, 18, 20, 22, 24. However, if the new grower finds using wiring difficult at first, plants can be scissor-trained. It takes a little longer to shape a mame bonsai with scissors, but this method is safest for a beginner.

Once a tree is in a small pot the trunk increases in girth very slowly. If possible, start with a plant having a thick trunk. Before transplanting it to the mame container, gradually reduce the size by repeated pruning of top and roots. If you want to grow the plant in a very tiny pot, 2-inch diameter or less, then use a rooted cutting or seedling and train the plant as it grows in the mame pot.

Philip B. Mullan

One-hand, or mame, bonsai of *Juniperus squamata* 'Prostrata', 12 years old. Trained in container 8 years.

Small-leaved forms of Japanese holly (*Ilex crenata*) can make fine mame.

Philip B. Mullan

34

When natural light is lacking

THE FLUORESCENT LIGHT GARDEN

Margery Craig

MANY indoor bonsai can be grown successfully under fluorescent light. In fact, plants often do better there because their cultural needs may be more easily met in the controlled environment of the light garden than in the varied conditions of windowsills around the home. Ideally, the light garden provides a winter growing area for subtropicals that have summered outdoors in full sunlight, but for apartment dwellers who have limited outdoor space, the lights can be used year round.

Plants to Grow

A great variety of plants will adapt to fluorescent light culture. Serissa grows and flowers continuously during the winter months, while gardenia (*G. jasminoides radicans*), Barbados-cherry *(Malpighia glabra)* and dwarf pomegranate *(Punica granatum nana)* also bloom, but less frequently. Plants native to very warm climates like bougainvillea bloom under fluorescents in late January; pyracanthas and azaleas from milder parts of the temperate zone bloom in early spring.

Among the evergreen plants that grow throughout the winter are podocarpus, various cypresses, Japanese box *(Buxus microphylla)*, weeping fig (*Ficus benjamina*), creeping fig (*Ficus pumila*), English ivy (*Hedera helix*), olive (*Olea europaea*), junipers and false-cypresses (*Chamaecyparis*). Other types of plants will rest for two or three months during the winter, then start active growth in early spring. Examples of these are Natal-plum (*Carissa grandiflora*),

willow-leaved fig *(Ficus neriifolia regularis)*, *Camellia sasanqua*, brush-cherry *(Syzygium paniculatum;* synonym, *Eugenia myrtifolia*), Chinese elm (*Ulmus parvifolia*), limeberry (*Triphasia triphylla*), lantana and hibiscus.

The light garden may also be used to start cuttings and seeds for indoor or outdoor bonsai. A clear plastic box containing a 2-inch layer of coarse, screened perlite makes a convenient cutting box as well as a good place to store fingertip-size mame bonsai during long weekends and vacations. The perlite, which is moistened, maintains a humid atmosphere but is sterile so that damping-off or other fungus growth is seldom a problem. If there are two or three small holes in the top and in the bottom of this box for air circulation and drainage, mame bonsai can be kept alive for a week or two without attention. As a cutting box, it rarely needs any care. After the initial watering when the cuttings are made, it should be checked monthly, but no additional water should be added unless the perlite is dry to the touch.

Design

The design of the light garden can be as varied and decorative as space and ingenuity allow. It has the great advantage of being flexible in size so that units may be added as desired. Commercial fluorescent units are available at garden centers but for those wishing to design their own, most of the necessary materials are available at hardware or building-supply stores.

35

An indoor light garden installed under
cabinets on a kitchen counter, handy to
sink and easy to clean.

In choosing the length of fluorescent
tubes, it is useful to remember that light
intensity diminishes at the ends of any
fluorescent tube. For this reason longer
tubes are more efficient than shorter
ones. The 48-inch tube is a convenient
basic unit and the light garden may be
made up of multiples of this readily available size.

A typical light system consists of two
48-inch tubes mounted in single strip fixtures spaced 6 inches apart on the underside of a shelf or stand 20 inches above a
table or the shelf below. Two standard
11- x 22-inch waterproof plastic plant
trays fit conveniently under each pair of
lamps. To give varied distance to the
lights for different size plants, one of the
trays may be set up 3-4 inches on an
overturned flat or on blocks of wood. The
ballast from the fixtures may be removed
and mounted separately to save space
and reduce heat in the plant area. A re-
flector above the lights is not required if
the shelf on which the tubes are mounted
is painted with super-white flat paint.

Green plants cannot use all wavelengths of visible light. The red and blue ends of the spectrum promote plant growth and flowering, so fluorescent tubes which provide greater light intensity in these areas will produce more lush growth. I have found that Verilux Tru-Bloom tubes are very satisfactory, as are the Gro-Lux Wide Spectrum bulbs. The improved deluxe cool white and warm white tubes now also have increased output in the wavelengths plants can use. For maximum growth the tops of the plants should be no more than 4-6 inches from the lights. An appliance timer set for 14-15 hours per day can be used to turn on the lights automatically.

Growth Requirements

The humidity required for healthy plant growth should be provided by placing a half-inch layer of pebbles in the bottom of the plant trays and keeping this covered with water. To prevent the soil from taking up this moisture, the pots should rest on a support above the level of the water. A convenient support may be made from "egg crate" nylon fluorescent light diffusers available at building supply stores. This is sawed to fit snugly into the tops of the plastic trays which taper and support the diffuser above the water level. If the temperature in the growing area ranges between 60-65°F this arrangement will provide sufficient humidity. Some plants require greater heat and humidity. This may be obtained by taping a 75°F heating cable in the bottom of the trays before the pebbles are added.

The final cultural requirement for successful light gardening with indoor bonsai is to have good air circulation both in the air around the plants and in the soil. The first need can best be met with small fans designed to run at low speed. One fan hung in each 48-inch unit moves enough air to keep the plants healthy. On the second point, the soil mix must be carefully prepared and proper attention given to watering only as often as the soil dries. This will vary with the size of the pot. Very small bonsai require water every day. Most larger plants need water only once or twice a week.

For indoor plants to thrive, the soil must drain very rapidly. To accomplish this, all the components in the soil mix should be screened and particles passing through a 1/16 inch mesh window screen should be discarded. A potting soil made up of two parts sharp coarse sand, one part near-neutral potting soil, and one part well-decayed compost is a good general mixture. Peat moss or acid potting soils should be avoided because some mild-climate plants grow in quite alkaline conditions in their natural habitat and may not do well in an acid potting mix even if lime is added. Barbados-cherry and bougainvillea are striking examples.

Fertilizer should be given only to those plants which are actively growing. Alternate use of fish emulsion (nutrients released slowly) and a water-soluble fertilizer (nutrients released quickly) works well. In general, employ a high-phosphate type of fertilizer for plants grown for their flowers, an acid type for azaleas and gardenias and an equal-analysis type for evergreen and deciduous trees grown for their foliage. Better results are obtained with frequent very dilute fertilization rather than full strength once-a-month applications. One-eighth teaspoon per gallon can be used at every other watering.

Finally, pest control is best dealt with by prevention. When plants are brought in from summer growing they should be inspected carefully and given a precautionary spraying with malathion. Any new plants acquired during the winter should be quarantined for a week in a sunny window to make certain they don't harbor any pests. If there is an outbreak of aphids, white flies or spider mites, the most common indoor pests, the synthetic pyrethrenoid sprays will usually control them. Water-emulsion aerosols such as Hyponex Bug Control do not damage foliage and are safe to use indoors provided label instructions are carefully followed.

For more ideas on light garden design and new improvements in indoor culture the Indoor Light Garden Society of America publication offers a wealth of information. Address: 128 West 58th Street, New York, New York 10019.

Start with character . . .

KINGSVILLE DWARF BOX AND SERISSA

Albert J. Lake

INDOOR BONSAI, outdoor bonsai, "instant" bonsai, mame bonsai—whatever! The prime factor is to find a decent tree or plant to work with. Some plants will never make a bonsai, others can be turned and wired into a presentable or even a good one. The best way to make a proper bonsai is to find a plant with at least some measure of character to start with.

The average garden center seldom offers much in the way of proper bonsai material for indoors. Therefore, the enthusiast must seek out a rare plant nursery or a bonsai establishment, or inquire among members of bonsai clubs, horticultural societies and arboreta. The satisfaction and excitement of finding good material more than justifies the time spent.

Kingsville Dwarf boxwood (*Buxus microphylla* 'Compacta') may be rather difficult to find in garden centers*, but it is probably the aristocrat of all indoor bon-

sai. This magnificent plant, generally petite in size, with its tiny leaves, remarkable branching and aged-looking bark is superb in every respect. It was introduced many years ago by the late H. J. Hohman of Kingsville Nurseries in Maryland and has steadily gained the favor of bonsai enthusiasts.

Kingsville Dwarf box is extremely slow growing. It is not particularly fussy about soil so long as there is good drainage and good light. Partial shade or filtered sunlight is best, although once acclimated in the home it can get along nicely with no direct sunshine at all. Growth may amount to no more than a quarter- or half-inch a year. New leaves are a handsome light green, contrasting delightfully with the darker older foliage. When

*—ed. For a list of mail-order sources see Brooklyn Botanic Garden Handbook No. 63, *1200 Trees and Shrubs—Where to Buy Them.*

Marge Craig

Kingsville dwarf box, only 17 inches high after many years in training.

Eighteen inch Kingsville
dwarf box, from nursery
stock 8 years ago. Needs
cool window in winter.

Gregg R. Wadleigh

grown as an outdoor shrub it is hardy in
most of the northern states, but the
leaves will bronze in winter. As an indoor
bonsai the foliage remains green year
round. Often, perfectly charming bonsai
can be fashioned from the Kingsville
Dwarf box by pruning and pinching
alone—no wiring needed!

A fifty-year-old specimen is only about
20 inches tall; eight- to twelve-year plants
may reach 6 or 7 inches in height; four-
year plants are about 3 inches tall. Spread
is likely to be wider than the height. Regardless of size, Kingsville Dwarf never
fails to enchant all who see it.

Kingsville Dwarf is one of the relatively few plants from the cool-
temperate zone that makes a good indoor
bonsai. It is derived from an Oriental
species which should not be confused
with the common box (*Buxus sempervirens*).

Serissa

In contrast, a fast grower for indoor bonsai is serissa (*S. foetida*) in its various
forms. It can grow from a cutting to a 15-
inch tall miniature tree in two years or
less, and can be shaped and pruned along
the way. In fact, after reaching the desired size, it must be pinched frequently
to maintain its bonsai shape.

The very small, glossy leaves of serissa
resemble a dwarf box, but this shrub from
southeast Asia is a member of the large
Coffee Family (Rubiaceae). A variant
with very narrow yellow leaf margins, is
quite distinctive. There is also a double-
flowered form commonly known as the
snow-rose whose tiny white blossoms do
indeed look like roses. Serissa and its
forms are gaining favor steadily among
indoor bonsai enthusiasts—and rightfully
so.

39

New bonsai from old favorites . . .

CAMELLIAS AND GARDENIAS

Lynn Perry Alstadt

MOST people think of camellias as being too large in flower and leaf to make good bonsai. This is true of the common varieties grown in mild-climate gardens the world over for their conspicuous saucer-like blossoms and bold, shining green foliage. However, did you know there are genetic miniatures available from specialist dealers? They make prime bonsai candidates if you have a home greenhouse or unheated sun porch where the air is cool and humid.

My favorite miniature camellia is 'Bob's Tinsie', which a friend brought me from California six or seven years ago. The growth habit of the plant is compact and very upright. It begins to flower in a cool greenhouse (55°F) in early December and continues until April. As soon as it has flowered, the new growth, which is light green with bronze edges, begins to appear. I pinch it back early to two new leaves. The plant will then develop both vegetative and flower buds in the axils of the two remaining leaves for the following year. Too many flower buds usually

form, and I remove about half. Even so, last year 'Bob's Tinsie' had fifty blossoms.

My miniature camellias are transplanted every two years, when new growth begins. The potting mix is one part peat moss, one part terra green (or sand), and two parts soil. The roots are not cut drastically during repotting. I do it gradually over two or three potting sessions (four to six years).

Gardenias

There is a dwarf gardenia (*G. jasminoides radicans*) that I grow as an indoor bonsai, too. It has long, narrow, shiny leaves and creamy white flowers about the size of a fifty-cent piece. This plant is a compact, vigorous grower which must be pruned hard yearly to maintain its bonsai form. Although it is an evergreen, the three-year old leaves are shed after the plant flowers in June. Cuttings root readily in a mixture of half sand and half peat, which is also a good growing medium.

Philip B. Mullan

Gardenia jasminoides radicans, natural dwarf about 4 years old, 3 years in training, unfinished form.

Camellia sasanqua, in training 7 years, informal upright form.

Gardenia jasminoides radicans has attractive golden yellow fruits in autumn, but only if time has been taken in spring to cross-pollinate the flowers with a small brush. This must be done over a period of ten days to three weeks because the plant doesn't bloom all at once. However, it's worth it because a second season of interest is gained thereby.

Growing a gardenia in the house is sometimes difficult. Either it's too hot and dry, or too cold and wet, or too drafty. Such an array of possible problems! However, there is a way to grow the gardenia satisfactorily without consigning it to a greenhouse. Set the container in a clear polyethylene bag and draw the bag about half way up around the plant. Keep in an east window in winter. (If a south window must be used, place the plant back several feet from the sill to prevent overheating.) The bag treatment conserves moisture and excludes drafts, thus helping to keep temperatures sufficiently even for good growth.

Care

As with all my bonsai, I spend extra time pruning the new growth of camellias and gardenias so they won't have to be wired. However, if it becomes desirable to wire them, I wait until flowering stops and new growth begins to mature. The wire is kept on for only a brief period (three to six weeks) because of the plants' vigor and the danger of the wire marking the branches. I rewire then only if necessary. A time-release fertilizer is applied in spring and again in autumn.

Pests, notably aphids and cottony scale, appear from time to time. Both are bothersome to eradicate. I apply an appropriate insecticide if the infestation is heavy. If it is light, a water spray with mild soap, followed by a rinse, is usually enough. Maintaining bonsai plants in a clean condition all of the time is the best preventive measure against insects and disease, so as a weekly procedure I turn on a bonsai microspray watering attachment a little harder than I would for normal watering and aim the spray up underneath the foliage. Snails like to eat the flowers of the camellias in my greenhouse. I don't care to have poisonous baits around and have found that saucers of beer control these pests well.

A final note. Both camellias and gardenias benefit from spending the summer outdoors in the filtered light of high-branched trees.

41

A varied group for indoor bonsai

THE ORNAMENTAL FIG

J. Richard Bowen

THE GENUS FICUS, which is best known among temperate-climate gardeners for the common fig, includes many ornamental species of trees, shrubs and vines from the warmer parts of the world. Some of them rank with the largest plants known to man, others are only tiny creepers. The ones suitable for indoor bonsai need good light, warmth and humidity.

In the winter I keep my ficus and other indoor bonsai on card tables in a corner of a bedless bedroom where there is light from a side window and above through a 3-foot-square skylight. The plants sit in pots on plastic trays that contain water. I gave up the idea of using pebbles for a base as it is too difficult to keep the trays clean. The water level is below the drain holes of the pots, of course, so plants don't become waterlogged.

I have a five-tree grove of the willow-leaved fig (*Ficus neriifolia regularis*) that requires frequent but light feeding year round. There is also a Chinese banyan (*F. retusa*) on a piece of lava; it needs very

little fertilizer. A loose. gritty soil mix seems to work well for these plants. It consists of half sand and half garden loam (pasteurized), with only the coarser pebbles of sand being used after screening. The fertilizer I favor is fish emulsion (usually 5-5-1).

The ficus grove has given us particular pleasure, but it does have an occasional problem. Every spring it is attacked by spider mites, which are very tiny. They are virtually colorless and shed their skins like snakes. These minute creatures clutter up the leaves and look dreadful—under a microscope, that is. A way I have found to control them is to dunk the plant in mild, soapy (not detergent) water, and thoroughly rinsing. I place the pot in a plastic bag and wrap the end around and over the soil to prevent it from spilling out, and then I invert the plant in the water. It is a little difficult because the top of the bonsai is 22 inches above the container, but dunking in this manner washes off the mites.

Philip B. Mullan

Two-tree slanting style of weeping fig is symbolic of husband and wife. Four years old, 1 year in training.

Five-tree grove of
willow-leaved fig, in
training 6 years.
Author's collection.

Peter Chvany

Weeping fig, 28 inches, in training
15 years but redesigned 3 years ago
as indoor bonsai.

Beautiful and easy to grow . . .

THE MYRTLE OF THE ANCIENTS

Elizabeth N. Hume

WOULD you like an uncommon indoor bonsai that is beautiful and easy to grow? Then search the garden marts and florist shops until you find the common myrtle (*Myrtus communis*). It is usually a small but very leafy potted plant of deepest green, with a scattering of bead-like buds and dainty white, mildly fragrant flowers. The evergreen leaves when crushed have a strongly aromatic, spicy scent—somewhat reminiscent of an Oriental bazaar—and are utterly delightful. For added interest the plants form bluish-black berries when growing conditions are good. They are reportedly non-poisonous, but take no chances.

If you plan to create an upright miniature tree form, be sure to check the main trunk and the placement of the branches before purchasing a young plant. Actually myrtle wood is strong and resilient—nearly as lithe as willow, and it adapts well to almost any style that is desired. New growth sprouts from the trunk at times, quite unexpectedly. The new shoot or shoots can, if you wish, become well placed branches in a surprisingly short time. This is another plus for a most obliging little tree, particularly if you are new to bonsai and have made a mistake in pruning.

It is possible but not likely that you will one day come upon a large and fine specimen in a nursery greenhouse. Chances are it won't be for sale, for with it would go sentiment and symbolism from an old family enterprise. If you are young, start your own, grow it without benefit of much pruning, and no doubt you will not part with yours either in twenty or thirty years.

History and Legend

Myrtle originated in West Asia, the very cradle of civilization. It symbolized peace at the burial of the dead in many of the Middle East countries, and it is mentioned in the Old Testament in the Bible: "And he stood among the myrtle trees" Zechariah I.

In Greek mythology, Venus, goddess of love, youth and beauty, is portrayed rising from the sea bearing a spray of myrtle. To this day it is traditional in many European countries to include a sprig of myrtle in the bridal bouquet.

Historically, myrtle crowned the heads of Roman generals home from the wars and garlands decorated their temples and perfumed their halls of revelry. It is conjectural that these same generals introduced the myrtle to the shores of England and the Channel Isles. Later, very much later, these towns and islands supplied quantities of cut myrtle boughs in large bundles to Covent Garden in London, where they were sold to decorate the massive mantles and perfume the sleeping quarters of many a stately home in the 17th and early 18th centuries. No lady of the time was without her myrtle. Enough perhaps of history, legend and lore. Our subject is indoor bonsai, and this new way of growing plants is of consuming interest to more and more people.

Care

Using bonsai principles and techniques, city-dwellers can now achieve decorative results of which they can be very proud. For the traditional bonsai person the joy of growing and creating with subtropical

44

Yuji Yoshimura

Small-leaved myrtle (*Myrtus communis* 'Microphylla') group planting. The tallest is 15 inches.

material the year-round is indeed a whole new field.

The common myrtle is of easy culture for the beginner. I would suggest growing it for a while as a house plant before repotting or styling. Get to know its requirements and study its artistic possibilities. The chances are that the plant will flower best for you if it has good light and is not allowed to dry out thoroughly between waterings. Watch for scale insects and other pests and control them with an appropriate insecticide according to directions on the label.

When you do transplant, use a potting mixture of loam, humus, a generous amount of sharp sand for drainage and a pinch of slow-release fertilizer.

Myrtle responds quickly to feeding whenever a burst of fresh new green is desired, but it is able to cope with minimum care and maintain its attractiveness throughout the winter months—marking time, of course, for a spring display of foliage that is truly beautiful. During the active growing season an occasional application of a balanced fertilizer having a 12-15% nitrogen formula (diluted in twice as much water as the package recommends) keeps the leaves in good color.

Because the common myrtle has been grown since the earliest of times, it should be no surprise that a number of cultivated varieties have occurred. There are at least two with variegated foliage, the one with

45

Myrtus communis 'Microphylla' twin trunk, 21 inches high.

the smallest leaves being especially choice. Each makes a fine display against a dark background and gives the striking illusion of a plant in bloom—or a tree in sunshine.

Size is not the most important criterion for an excellent bonsai, but the perfect tree of small stature is indeed the ultimate aim of many connoisseurs. The common myrtle is a splendid candidate for this purpose. The tiny leaves of a well formed plant bear silent testimony of tender loving care throughout the year.

Final note: It might be wise to mention that periwinkle (*Vinca minor*), a hardy ground-cover plant, is sometimes called myrtle, too. How or why it received this misleading name is a mystery to me, for it bears no resemblance and is not even a member of the same botanical family. To avoid confusion when ordering the true myrtle of the Ancients, be sure to include its botanical name, *Myrtus communis*.

Why not . . .

HERBS AND SUCCULENTS
Eleanor Thatcher

BONSAI techniques are being applied to all sorts of plants these days. Herbs and succulents are among the ones that have caught our interest at the Kathryn S. Taylor Greenhouse of the Massachusetts Horticultural Society in Waltham. This may come as a surprise to readers who think of bonsai in traditional Japanese terms. Succulents, which are often characterized by thick, fleshy leaves, represent in good part the deserts of the world, while herbs evoke an image of parched Mediterranean lands. Yet, both groups are tremendously varied, and the innovative grower has many choices.

Herbs

Herbs present delightful possibilities. It might be stressed first that we are not restricting the word 'herb' to its botanical meaning (*i.e.*, a non-woody plant) but are including some woody or semi-woody plants that have traditionally been associated with kitchen, medicine or fragrance. For indoor bonsai select the herbs that do have a woody stem, such as the versatile rosemary (*Rosmarinus officinalis*), which over the years has had at least a hundred other uses—many of them less orthodox. This ancient herb, the symbol of remembrance, is noted for its aromatic, very narrow, dark green leaves and small blue flowers, which appear in spring. Rosemary may be grown in a south window or, even better, under artificial light. Plants can be trimmed and shaped into interesting art forms in only a year or two. Variety 'Prostratus' is also choice for our purposes.

If you succeed with rosemary, you might like to try some of the other classic Mediterranean herbs that are part woody and have refined foliage. Several of them have been popular in Elizabethan-type knot gardens as dwarf, clipped hedges. Among the appropriate candidates are: germander (*Teucrium chamaedrys*), with small, shiny green, notched leaves; lavender (*Lavandula* spp.), narrow gray foliage; sage (*Salvia officinalis*), larger gray-green leaves; santolina with either silvery foliage (*S. chamaecyparissus*) or green (*S. virens*); common thyme (*Thymus vulgaris*); and winter savory (*Satureja montana*). Some of these have flower spikes rising above the leaves—best cut them off in the training stage. Lemon-verbena (*Aloysia triphylla;* formerly *Lippia citriodora*), a native of South America, might also be tried.

All of the above plants may be expected to perform best in a cool greenhouse in winter, or on a sunporch. They also do well grown under artificial light in a cold room. If these conditions can't be provided, try a southern window in a room which is cool at night. Herbs are not true house plants for the most part but can cope if you are able to give the proper environment.

Herbal Trees and Shrubs

Trees and larger-growing shrubs have been used in herb gardens since ancient times. They were trained, shaped, clipped and sheared to form various patterns. Because some species were not hardy in frost zones, they had to be brought indoors and grown in tubs and boxes.

A few of them, such as the calamondin orange (*Citrus mitis*) and sweet-olive (*Osmanthus fragrans*) were brought from the Orient to the West, where they eventually became associated with herb gardens, but most were of European or Eurasian origin. They include English or common box (*Buxus sempervirens*) and English holly (*Ilex aquifolium*), neither of which is particularly Anglo-Saxon despite their vernacular names; also certain junipers (for their religious associations), myrtle (*Myrtus communis*) (see page 44), and the olive of commerce (*Olea europaea*). English ivy (*Hedera helix*)

George Hull

Jade plant (*Crassula argentea*) before bonsai styling.

George Hull

Same jade plant after pruning and repotting.

also has a similar association. Because most of these plants have been cultivated for many years, in some cases from the time of man's earliest memories, it is not surprising that a number of variants exist. The innovative bonsai grower will want to seek out small-leaved or naturally dwarf forms.

Succulents

Some succulents—with a little bit of imagination, look like small pine trees. Others gradually drop their lower leaves giving an attractive bonsai effect as their trunks develop. Many, such as the miniature geraniums, which are succulents or herbs depending on your view, have attractive flowers. Small succulents lend themselves well to mame (miniature bonsai) or saikei (group plantings).

At the Taylor Greenhouse most of the succulents used for bonsai come from the Stonecrop Family (Crassulaceae). Certain crassulas have been popular house plants since Victorian times. One often sees large old specimens that have passed through several generations, handed down from parent to child. To me, crassulas seem perfectly suitable as an upright style of bonsai.

My favorite succulent is *Aeonium domesticum*, which apparently has no common name although it is grown by the thousands in southern California and in greenhouses around the country. Probably a hybrid from the Canary Islands, this small plant of the Stonecrop Family forms rosettes of leaves on single or branching stems. As it matures, it drops the lower leaves and takes on the appearance of a bonsai tree.

48

Other appropriate succulents include *Crassula lycopodioides*, *C. pseudo-lycopodioides* and *C. tetragona*. Best known, of course, is the jade plant (*C. argentea*) (see page 7). All of these are from South Africa.

Two other plants from South Africa deserve a word here. One of the most distinctive for bonsai purposes is *Portulacaria afra*, a very stout member of the Purslane Family which elephants are accustomed to browse upon in the wild—hence the common name, elephant bush. It has a variegated form, too. The other species that makes an interesting bonsai-like plant is *Trichodiadema bulbosum*, a representative of the Iceplant Family with carrot-shaped roots.

Culture

Despite their different origins and appearance, herbs and succulents have several things in common when their cultivation is considered. Most of them grow best in good light, actually very strong light. Neither is harmed by summer heat; in fact they thrive on it. In winter the herbs are best kept on the cool side at night and are more difficult to grow as house plants. Water requirements for both are light to moderate depending on seasons of growth. Don't let succulents or herbs sit in water for any length of time.

We use our own general potting mix, which consists of two parts garden soil (pasteurized), one part peat moss and one part perlite or sand. To this a little dolomitic limestone and a complete granular fertilizer (5-10-10 or 5-10-5) are added. However, a commercial soil mix works well too, and is easier for the apartment dweller to use.

Apply a balanced low-nitrogen fertilizer at half strength (or less) when plants are in active growth. If you are an "organic" gardener, try fish emulsion at half strength. If the growing medium is sterile, best employ a liquid fertilizer, not a granular one. In all cases, tend to under-feed than overfeed. One final note: avoid using the insecticide malathion on members of the Stonecrop Family; severe damage may result.

Philip B. Mullan

Twelve year old olive (*Olea europaea*), an herbal tree.

Distinctive subjects for indoor bonsai

100 PLANTS FROM A TO Z

Constance T. Derderian

SOME are easy, others require a little more effort. All of them make distinctive indoor bonsai. Find the ones that suit you. Don't forget that houses in warmer parts of the United States are often built to exclude sun. Houses in northern climes admit more light.

Many of the plants listed below can stand lower temperatures than coded. Temperatures in the code represent an optimum.

Most plants need very good light to flower and fruit well. If you can't provide it, select plants primarily grown for their foliage—or install an artificial light unit.

Plants will usually grow more rapidly with added humidity.

If leaves fall because plants are over- or underwatered, don't panic. Keep watering lightly and the chances are that new foliage will grow again in several weeks. Also, remember that newly purchased plants, or recently repotted ones, often suffer shock in the home. Treat the patients with patience.

In general, when repotting is necessary, do it in midwinter or very early spring before the plant is actively growing.

The following code is for winter care. Summer temperatures can—and will—be warmer. The plants in the following list are evergreen or nearly so, except where noted.

The Winter Code

1—House temperatures of 60° night to 75° F day. Good light, not necessarily sun.
2—House temperatures of 60° night to 75° F day. Provide as much sun as possible.
3—Cooler by about 10° than normal house temperatures. Give good light or some sun.
4—Difficult to grow in the average home. Learn about plant's needs. (A combination of numbers, *e.g.*, 3-2, indicates

that the plant grows best at a cool temperature but can adapt to a somewhat warmer one.)

Acacia baileyana—Golden Mimosa. (3). An Australian tree noted for its feathery silver-blue foliage. Give it a cool winter temperature. Don't repot every year.

Acacia farnesiana—Sweet Acacia (2). A South American species which adapts to warm winter temperature in the home better than the preceding. Both have fragrant flowers.

Araucaria heterophylla (excelsa)— Norfolk Island-pine (1). One of the best known tall trees of the subtropical landscape. In the home it tolerates winter heat and dryness.

Bougainvillea species and cultivars. (2). What visitor to mild climates doesn't admire this beautiful climbing shrub? Plants flower best in strong light. In the home bougainvillea will drop leaves if too wet or cold.

Bucida buceras— Geometry-tree, Black-olive. (1). Often grown as a street tree in Florida. This Caribbean species is almost self-shaping as a bonsai.

Bucida spinosa—Dwarf Black-olive. (1). Keep very moist. Root prune lightly in midsummer or midwinter. More difficult to find in the trade than the preceding, but charming to grow. See page 65.

Bursera simaruba—Gumbo Limbo or Tourist-tree (because it is always red and peeling). (1). A Caribbean species grown for its interesting red bark. In the Deep South it roots as easily as a willow does in the North—just stick a young branch into the ground and keep it watered. As an indoor bonsai it tolerates winter heat and dry soil.

Buxus harlandii. (1). A relatively little-known dwarf Chinese box which tolerates heat and dryness.

Buxus microphylla 'Compacta'—Kingsville Dwarf Box. (1). Don't overwater or overfertilize. (Also see page 38.) Same for *B. m. japonica* and *B. m. koreana.*

Calliandra emarginata—Dwarf Red Powder-puff. (1). Leaves fold up at night. Flowers in ratio to light. Same for *C. haematocephala (inaequilatera)* and *C. surinamensis.*

Camellia japonica. (3 or 2). Give it acid soil. Buds drop if too warm or dry. See page 40.

Camellia sasanqua. (3). Do not overwater.

Carissa grandiflora—Natal-plum. (1). A familiar boy-proof hedge in mild climates because of dense, thorny growth. Dwarf, small-leaved cultivars of this South African shrub with rounded-oval, sharp-tipped leaves have become popular in the southern California and Florida landscapes. Old plants resent heavy root pruning. In the home Natal-plum grows best in strong light. Sun is needed for the fragrant white flowers and for the edible fruits, which are red and have a pleasant flavor. Also see page 65.

Cassia marilandica—Wild Senna. (1). A native medicinal plant of the eastern United States with semi-woody stems and refined compound leaves. The yellow, pea-like flowers appear almost continuously when wild senna is grown in partial sun.

Chaenomeles japonica—Japanese Flowering Quince. (3). Can grow in warmer temperature if humidity is good. Deciduous. Strong light is needed to produce blossoms, which are bright orange.

Chamaecyparis pisifera 'Plumosa'—Plume-cypress, ''Faith-tree'', (3-2). Although the false-cypresses are mostly from the cool-temperate regions and are associated with traditional bonsai, some will perform well indoors. This Japanese variant with delicate frond-like branchlets will grow in slightly warmer winter temperatures than indicated by the code if the foliage is frequently misted.

Chamaecyparis pisifera 'Squarrosa'—Moss-cypress. (3). Has small feathery silver needles. Same culture as above.

Cinnamomum camphora—Camphor-tree. (2). An Oriental species often grown as

Philip B. Mullan

Plume-cypress (*Chamaecyparis pisifera* 'Plumosa'), clasping style. Six years old, still in training. It will take another five years for the roots to become exposed.

Otaheite orange (*Citrus taitensis*), left, 19 years in training, protects a little companion, *Juniperus formosana*, 11 years old.

a street tree in very mild parts of the United States. Foliage is dense and glossy. Leaves are somewhat large but can be reduced by bonsai techniques. The camphor of commerce is distilled from this tree.

Cissus rhombifolia—Grape-ivy. (1). An attractive South American vine which nearly everyone sooner or later grows as a house plant. It tolerates heat, dry soil, poor light and inexperienced gardeners. Give the grape-ivy some tender loving care and see how beautifully it responds.

Citrus species—Calamondin, Marco Orange, Otaheite Orange, Seville Orange, Meyer Lemon, Grapefruit, etc. (3-2). Give them acid soil and fertilize regularly. Once their needs are understood they are easy to grow.

Clerodendrum thomsoniae—Bleeding-heart Glorybower. (1). Shrubby West African vine noted for its red flowers, long stamens and white calyces. Long period of effectiveness. Keep plants well watered and pinch new vining growth to maintain shape.

Coccoloba uvifera—Sea-grape. (1). A bold coastal fixture in mild climates. The shrub is tolerant of heat and dry soil. Do not over-water. Also see page 69.

Conocarpus erectus—Buttonwood. (1). A native shrub or tree of southern Florida, the Bahamas and West Indies. Slender, leathery, gray-green foliage. Plants must be well watered. Do not repot every year. Trained more satisfactorily by pinching than wiring. Also see page 66.

Cotoneaster species and cultivars. (3). Seek out the low-growing, small-leaved sorts such as *C. microphyllus* and its variety *cochleatus*. They make excellent mame.

Cryptomeria japonica—Cryptomeria. (3-2). This monarch of the Japanese forests wouldn't appear to be a candidate for indoor bonsai, but it can be grown. One of the most beautiful conifers. Plants sold as *C. j. nana* usually adapt more easily than the species. Give them as much humidity as they can get.

Cuphea hyssopifolia—False-heather. (1). A dwarf shrub from Mexico and Guatemala with small, very narrow leaves. The dainty purplish-rose flowers bloom all winter with a little sun. Great for mame. Don't let the plant dry out—it isn't a very good convalescent.

Cupressus arizonica—Arizona Cypress. (3). Several of the true cypresses, which are mostly from mild climates, can be grown as indoor bonsai. Keep the humidity high and don't let them dry out. The reduced light intensity in the home may cause the foliage of Arizona cypress to become gray-green instead of glaucous.

Cupressus macrocarpa—Monterey Cypress. (3-2). Nature does the pruning better on the windswept Monterey peninsula of California than we can in the home, but this is a relict species well worth growing. The foliage is bright green. Again, keep the humidity high and don't allow plants to dry out.

Distylium racemosum. (2) A dense slow-growing foliage shrub from Japan, where it can be a tree eighty feet tall, somewhat resembling Japanese privet but botanically akin to the witch-hazel. Planted mainly in California gardens but worthy of trial if you can locate a young plant.

Eugenia uniflora—Surinam-cherry. (2-1). A shrub or small tree, originally from Brazil but widely grown in Florida, especially as a hedge. The foliage is glossy, with new growth being bright red. Excellent light is needed indoors for the development of the deep red fruits, which are edible. Give this plant slightly acid soil.

Eurya japonica. (2) Attractive shrub grown for its leathery deep green foliage. In the home keep the plant warm in winter and always well drained.

Ficus aurea—Strangler Fig. (1). A common tree of southern Florida, noted for its ability to subdue nearby competitors. Like many figs it develops aerial rootlets. In the home it tolerates heat and dryness. The leaves reduce drastically in size when strangler fig is grown as a bonsai. There are more than 600 species of ficus so the home grower is faced with many choices.

Ficus benjamina—Weeping Fig. (1). A well-known house plant in the North, a

Three sea-grapes (*Coccoloba uvifera*). Left: collected seedling, in container 1½ years. Center: started from seed 10 years ago, in container six years. Right: from nursery stock, in container 2 years.

Gregg R. Wadleigh

massive tree in the Deep South. As a bonsai do not overwater. This remarkable species from India may eventually develop aerial roots. A heavy crown encourages development. It withstands heavy top and root pruning.

Ficus diversifolia—Mistletoe Fig. (2). Familiar house and patio plant with distinctive thick-textured leaves resembling inch-wide teardrops. This shrub from southern Asia is almost always in fruit. The fruit is small and greenish-yellow, and has character even if it is not colorful. Open, twisted branching. Of easy culture.

Ficus neriifolia regularis—Willow-leaved Fig. (1). Graceful tree from the Celebes and Moluccas with lax branches. As an indoor bonsai it develops aerial rootlets in time. Tolerant of heat, poor light and dry soil.

Philip B. Mullan

Ficus pumila minima—Creeping Fig. (1). A dainty small-leaved climber derived from a species that is native to Japan, China and Australia. Foliage almost heart-shaped. The plant is excellent for mame but is a slow grower.

Ficus retusa nitida—Indian-laurel or Banyan. (1). On visits to Florida, northern house-plant hobbyists are sometimes shocked to see the immense dimensions this tree can attain in the mild-climate garden. Still, it's an excellent glossy-textured indoor foliage plant. Even as a bonsai it may develop aerial rootlets in time. Indian-laurel stands heavy pruning. (See *F. benjamina* re: aerial roots.)

Fortunella hindsii—Hong Kong Wild Kumquat. (3). A spiny little tree with leathery foliage and very small orange-red fruit. Allow it to become slightly dry between waterings, which should be thorough. Give the same care to Nagami kumquat (*F. margarita*).

Gardenia jasminoides radicans. (1). Beware of temperature extremes. Requires good humidity. See page 40. *G. thunbergia* (3-1) is better in slightly cooler temperatures. Repot in midwinter.

Grevillea robusta—Silk-oak. (2). Tall-growing, weak-wooded Australian tree with attractive foliage, frequently planted in California and Florida gardens for a quick effect. As an indoor bonsai, wire it when young and pliable because the branches eventually become brittle.

Guaiacum officinale—Lignum Vitae, Holywood. (2). Dense-growing Caribbean tree noted for its beautiful whitish-gray bark and very hard wood. Give it warm winter conditions and

Two-tree planting of Arizona cypress (*Cupressus arizonica*) in training 4 years. Grown from a cutting taken 8 years ago.

Mistletoe fig (*Ficus diversifolia*) in fruit. Wired in the cascade style and grown as a bonsai for 3 years, it measures approximately 12 inches across. The botanical name of this plant has recently been changed to *Ficus deltoidea,* but it will likely be a few years before this becomes commonly used in the trade.

grow it in the best possible light for its flowers, which are true blue. Train lignum vitae by pruning rather than wiring.

Hedera helix—English ivy. (1). Many small-leaved cultivars are available. Excellent for mame.

Hibiscus rosa-sinensis cooperi. (2). Striking plant for its variegated narrow leaves—a kaleidoscope of red, white and green. Flowers small, red. Allow the plant to become a little dry between waterings.

Hibiscus rosa-sinensis 'Snow Queen'. (1-2). The foliage is marbled in white, the flowers are rose pink. Grow in bright light for best leaf color and to produce blossoms.

Ilex aquifolium 'Angustifolia'—Narrow-leaved English Holly. (3). A very attractive cultivar with tight bushy growth and lustrous dark green foliage. The spiny leaves are one inch long and about 1/4 inch across. Keep winter temperature low and humidity high.

Ilex crenata 'Helleri'. (3). This Japanese holly is a popular garden shrub in many parts of the country because of its small, dense, deep green foliage and low mounded growth habit. When grown as a bonsai it is better shaped by pruning than wiring because the branches are brittle. The same with *I. c.* 'Microphylla'.

Ilex vomitoria—Yaupon Holly. (1). A southern holly with lustrous, rather small leaves. Pistillate (female) plants have red fruits if pollinated. A diminutive cultivar, 'Stokes Dwarf', resembles *Ilex crenata* 'Helleri'. When transplanting yaupon, prune the roots lightly and pot up quickly.

Ixora javanica—Jungle-Geranium. (2). Rugged hedge shrub in Florida with waxy reddish long-lasting flowers. Give it acid soil. Tolerant of poor light for growth but needs good light for bloom. 'Nor-nel', a dwarf ixora, is great for smaller bonsai.

Jacaranda mimosifolia (acutifolia). (2). Deciduous Brazilian tree planted throughout the milder parts of the world for its showy lavender-blue flowers and lacy bipinnate leaves. It is difficult to achieve flowers on the terminals and keep a good bonsai form because of the pruning involved, so grow jacaranda mainly for its foliage.

Jasminum dichotomum—Pinwheel Jasmine. (2). Climbing West African shrub with lustrous foliage and fragrant white flowers that open at night. It stands root and top pruning well. *Jasminum rex*, from Thailand, has larger scentless flowers appearing sporadically all year. Give it a warm winter temperature.

Juniperus procumbens 'Nana'. (3-1). This excellent dwarf form of the Japanese garden juniper stands heavy pruning as a bonsai. Keep the foliage thinned out and if the plant is grown under warm conditions watch out for red spider. *J. squamata* 'Prostrata' (3), with very similar growth habit, also tolerates heavy pruning. Do not overwater. *J. chinensis sargentii* is less satisfactory indoors. All of these junipers perform best in the home with cool winter temperatures and high humidity. They are essentially outdoor, temperate zone plants.

Lagerstroemia indica—Crape-myrtle. (3-2). One of the best-known tall deciduous summer-flowering shrubs of mild climates, but hardy outdoors to Long Island. Flowers, usually pink to red, also range from white to lavender. Mildew on foliage is a problem in California and the South but can be controlled in pot culture with a systemic fungicide. Dwarf cultivars and color forms of this southern Asian species have been named in recent years. In the home crape-myrtle adapts to cooler winter temperatures. It needs bright light to flower. Tolerates heavy pruning.

Lantana camara and other spp. (2). Northern indoor growers who coddle lantana are often surprised to find it a common weed in mild climates. Even so, it is a satisfactory bonsai in the home if the humidity can be kept high. Give the plant bright light if you want the attractive flowers to be abundant. Lantana tolerates dry soil; do not overwater. Pinch rather than wire.

Laurus nobilis—Bay. (3). This shrub is the true laurel of the ancient Greeks. In the home watch for spider mites. The leaves are slow to reduce in size.

Leptospermum scoparium—New Zealand Tea-tree. (2). The leaves of this shrub are needlelike and the flowers are sometimes reminiscent of miniature roses, although it is a member of the Myrtle Family. Numerous color forms have been named. Plants resent heavy root pruning and need good humidity in the home.

Ligustrum japonicum—Japanese Privet. (1-3). If a plant could sue for libel, the evergreen Japanese privet would take northern gardeners to court because of their calumny toward the genus, which is based entirely on the uninspiring deciduous sorts used for hedges in snowy areas.

Actually, Japanese privet, which Sun Belt gardeners know very well, is a good candidate for our purposes. True,

Philip B. Mullan

Hong Kong wild kumquat (*Fortunella hindsii*) in bonsai 17 years. Note the delicate, ½ inch, deep orange fruit.

Uprooted slanting style round-leaved Japanese privet (*Ligustrum japonicum* 'Rotundifolium') has spent half of its 30 years in bonsai training.

Philip B. Mullan

the leaves are a bit slow to reduce in size, but they will toe the line eventually. They are a rich and shiny green and this makes it worthwhile. If the thought of growing privet disturbs you, try 'Rotundifolium' (2)—it doesn't resemble one at all. Or, experiment with glossy privet (*L. lucidum*) (2), grown for its white flowers.

Lonicera nitida—Box honeysuckle. (2). Often planted as a hedge in milder parts of the United States, this shrub from western China has a good tight growth pattern and shapes easily. The creamy white flowers are fragrant, but the plant is worth growing as a bonsai for its refined foliage alone.

Malpighia coccigera—Singapore-holly. (1). A small shrub native to the West Indies despite its common name. One of the most frequently grown plants for indoor bonsai. The glossy leaves, which are tiny and spiny (some not at all), are always attractive, and the delicate light pink flowers appear sporadically year round. Don't overwater.

Malpighia glabra—Barbados-cherry. (1). A shrub grown in the Florida landscape for its ornamental merits and edible fruits, which have a high vitamin C content. It's splendid for a "weeping" bonsai style. Broken twigs will heal if not completely severed. See page 66. (*M. punicifolia* is similar but with inedible fruit.)

Myrsine africana—African-box. (2). Foliage shrub with dark green, almost rounded leaves that are little more than a quarter-inch wide when grown as a bonsai. Red stems enhance the effect.

Myrtus communis—Myrtle. (1-2). Can be grown in many styles, including mame. See page 44.

Nicodemia diversifolia—Indoor-oak. (1). Foliage shrub from Madagascar with somewhat wavy lobed leaves that are prominently veined. They reduce in size well. Tend to pinching rather than wiring.

Nothofagus cunninghamii—Tasmanian-beech. (3-2). A very striking, very small-leaved, very tall-growing tree in

57

its homeland. The biggest danger in the bonsai container is overwatering, but it shouldn't be allowed to dry out either.

Olea europaea—Olive. (1-2). Have you ever admired a neglected grove of gnarled old olive trees in Spain or Greece—or even California? Aged specimens have a character unmatched by any cool-climate fruit tree, except possibly the apple. As an indoor bonsai the olive is very tolerant of winter heat and dryness. Don't overwater it.

Pinus elliottii—Slash Pine. (2). See page 66.

Pinus halepensis—Aleppo Pine. (1). This species is tolerant of greater heat and dryness than practically any other pine. The needles are usually in twos and have a light green appearance. The tree isn't as refined as some of the northern pines but it can take indoor conditions—and that is what we are looking for. Do not repot every year.

Pinus thunbergii—Japanese Black Pine. (3). If you must have a traditional bonsai pine, this is one that can adapt to the indoor condition (cool room with good humidity and light, please). The bright green needles are in twos. Root prune lightly when repotting.

Pithecellobium unguis-cati—Cat's Claw or Black Bead. (2). Caribbean shrub or small tree with refined leathery bipinnate leaves and small yellow flowers. Remarkable claw-like seed pods. Member of the Bean Family. Shape by pruning.

Pittosporum tobira. (1-3). Dense shrub or small tree from milder parts of Japan and China. The closely set, leathery foliage is dark green, the flowers are white and scented. Often planted as an ornamental in the South and on the West Coast. Best shape it by pruning because of its growth pattern.

Podocarpus macrophyllus maki— Southern-yew. (1-3). Versatile, ultimately tall foliage shrub from milder parts of Japan and China. It is used in Florida and California gardens in basically the same way as the related but much smaller-leaved *Taxus* is in the North. Try it indoors. The southern-yew responds well to top pruning.

Psidium cattleianum—Strawberry-guava.

(2). Keep it well watered but not sopping wet. See page 67.

Punica granatum nana—Dwarf Pomegranate. (2-1). A much used plant for indoor bonsai and mentioned several places in this Handbook. Tend to shape the plant by pinching rather than pruning. Keep the humidity high if possible. If you aren't the bashful type bring it into the bathroom when you take a shower.

Pyracantha species—Firethorn. (2-1). Northern gardeners know one species, the scarlet firethorn (*P. coccinea*), which in its several cultivars is a vigorous grower with prolific orange-red fruits. There are other species from generally milder climates which are better suited for our purposes: narrow-leaved firethorn (*P. angustifolia*), orange-red fruits; Formosan firethorn (*P. koidzumii*), relatively large, vivid red or orange-red fruits; Chinese firethorn (*P. fortuneana;* synonym: *crenato-serrata*), small leaves and profuse little red fruits. All of them have attractive white flower clusters in spring.

When grown as indoor bonsai, the firethorns bear fruit which is very persistent, a trait that will be appreciated by outdoor gardeners whose bushes are often quickly stripped of bounty by carousing robins. In the home these recommended firethorns are tolerant of winter heat and dry soil. Performance seems better in slightly alkaline soil.

Quercus spp. (4-1). All of the true oaks are slow and difficult to grow indoors. Unless you are fairly experienced with bonsai best concentrate on other plants in this list. However, if you would like to try these noble trees, start with young plants; root prune lightly and not every year.

The oaks that have a reasonable chance for survival as indoor bonsai are species from warmer climates such as water oak (*Q. nigra*), a southern, nearly evergreen tree with variable, rich green leaves, or cork oak (*Q. suber*), a Mediterranean species which produces the cork of commerce. Southern live oak (*Q. virginiana*) and the coast live oak of California (*Q. ag-*

rifolia), two trees with haunting beauty, great character and strong regional associations, are possibilities, too. Give the water oak a moist clay soil, the others a rich, well-drained one.

Raphiolepis indica—India-hawthorn. (2). Attractive leathery-leaved shrub with white-to-pink flowers depending on cultivar (in California there are a number). Long blooming period. This member of the Rose Family from southern China also has persistent blue-black fruit. As an indoor bonsai it is slow growing and brittle to wire.

Rhododendron indicum and other Evergreen Azaleas. (3-2). Can be grown in pure peat moss. Acid soil required. There are a number of excellent cultivars. If I had to choose but one, it would be the shell-pink-flowered 'Coral Bells' (a kurume); Japanese satsukis are choice, too; many others.

Rosmarinus officinalis—Rosemary. (3) See page 47. Keep humidity high in winter and don't overwater.

Serissa foetida and forms. (2-1). See page 39. Tend to pinch instead of wire. Don't overfertilize. The variegated form is a little easier to grow than the others but will become leggy unless light is very good.

Sparmannia africana—African-hemp. (1). Fast-growing shrub with large linden-like leaves that reduce in size with bonsai treatment. It has white flowers with prominent "featherduster" stamens. There is also a double-flowered form. Shape the plant by frequent pinching.

Syzygium paniculatum (Eugenia paniculata australis)—Australian brush-cherry. (1). Slender, dense growing tree sometimes used for hedges in mild climates. New growth reddish. As an indoor bonsai it grows quickly and is easy to shape.

Taxodium distichum—Bald-cypress. (1-3). See page 67. In the home this deciduous southern tree requires a cooler,

(Continued on p. 75)

Philip B. Mullan

Serissa foetida in its double-flowered form is also called snow-rose. Its ¼ inch white blossoms and shiny, dark green leaves are reminiscent of a miniature gardenia.

59

Some guidelines for . . .

INDOOR BONSAI IN THE NORTH
Sigmund Dreilinger

FOR MANY YEARS I was a frustrated bonsai grower because my traditional bonsai could only be grown outdoors—and for seven to eight months of the year at best. Each November I would put them in their winter quarters where they would remain until March. I would check them from time to time during the winter but no real work could be done until spring. I missed not being with them those four months and looked for ways to extend my involvement throughout the year. That was how my interest in subtropical trees and shrubs for bonsai began.

For years I was told that there are few kinds of plants suitable for indoor bonsai. A skeptic, I began to experiment. I started with what are now some of the most commonly used materials, *Serissa foetida* and the holly-leaved *Malpighia coccigera*. I quickly discovered that just so much can be learned from reading and that there is no substitute for experience. Regardless of the variety of plant or its country of origin, the basic cultural requirements had to be ascertained and met before any success could be realized.

Window Growing With Natural Light

One of the primary requirements of virtually all bonsai is adequate light. Obtaining sufficient illumination in the home can be a problem. The ideal location for the most commonly used bonsai plants is a south-facing window unshaded by trees or buildings. If the grower is unable to provide a southern exposure, the use of artificial lighting should be seriously considered. This will be discussed in greater detail later in this article and on page 35.

Bonsai grown indoors on a windowsill are subject to different temperatures from bonsai grown elsewhere in the house. Regardless of what temperature is maintained in the home, temperatures are always slightly lower in window areas, and this must be taken into account when growing bonsai there. A lack of storm sash in the winter tends to lower these temperatures still further. Keep track of the variations in different windows and make a conscious effort to maintain the range between 60°F and 85°F. Fluctuations between these two extremes should prove satisfactory for most window-grown bonsai.

In the average home, the dry heat of winter causes great trauma for humidity-loving plants. Bonsai seem to suffer more than most from this lack of moisture in the air. Misting several times a day can help offset the damage done by dry air. In addition, if the bonsai are small enough and very portable, they can be brought into the bathroom when you shower or into the kitchen when you are washing the dishes. Both activities increase the moisture in the air.

Frequency of watering has to be adjusted to the temperature and humidity indoors as well as the growing medium of the bonsai. Outdoors, I use a 50/50 potting mix, by volume, of peat moss and sand. This is a quick-draining mix that, with the frequent addition of a water-soluble fertilizer (one-quarter strength), has worked well. Inside the house, this mix tends to dry out more rapidly and needs more attention. Small and shallow mame containers need watering once a day and occasionally more often. Some of the larger, deeper containers, however, can last forty-eight hours between waterings. Each container really should be checked individually, though, as different kinds of plants absorb water at different rates.

Artificial Lights

In the past twenty years great advances have been made in the lighting industry and a wide range of fluorescent tubes are now available to the homeowner. These innovations have largely done away with

Sigmund Dreilinger

Buttonwood (*Conocarpus erectus*) collected from Florida Keys by author. In training one year.

Siomund Dreilinoer

Satsuki azalea, 7 years old. In training 4 years.

the need for sunny windows. It is now possible to grow many kinds of bonsai, including the most light-loving, in the darkest corners of the house.

Because an even distribution of light is so important, I decided against using commercial fluorescent fixtures that concentrate the tubes in the center. Instead, I purchased 2 two-tubed strip fixtures. They were mounted on 20- x 48-inch exterior plywood panels that had been painted with a white enamel to increase their reflecting properties. The tubes were placed so that the outer ones were 3 inches in from the plywood edge. The inner tubes were in three inches beyond these. This left a 6-inch center area which received light from both sides and was therefore evenly lighted.

Indoors, the house heat plus the heat generated by the fluorescent ballasts raises the air temperature around the bonsai to approximately 75°F when the lights are on. At night, when the lights are off, and depending on the outside temperature, the window is opened to a greater or lesser degree. This serves to cool and ventilate the room so that the temperature drops from fifteen to twenty degrees below the day temperature. If the night temperature falls to 55°F, no harm is done. Those bonsai which are most sensitive to the cold should be placed in another area of the house where higher night temperatures prevail.

The humidity conditions for bonsai grown indoors under lights are somewhat different than for those grown indoors under natural light. In addition to the aforementioned dryness that prevails in most homes throughout the winter, fluorescent ballasts create a slight but additional heat. To combat this, plants must be misted regularly, sometimes as often as twice a day.

Bonsai grown indoors suffer far less from the vagaries of the weather than those grown outdoors. Indoors, watering is done as needed and does not depend on sometimes infrequent rains. Most of my bonsai are placed on pebbles in plastic trays under their lights, partly to retain excess drainage water and partly to cut down on frequency of watering. By plac-

ing water in the plastic trays to a depth of one-quarter inch, I find I can often leave my bonsai for from four to five days. By the third day most of the water will have evaporated from the tray, but it generally takes the soil another two days to dry out sufficiently to require more water.

My subtropical bonsai are put outdoors for the summer and brought in during early autumn before night temperatures drop below 55°F. Then I turn on the artificial lights for twelve hours a day and gradually decrease the length to ten hours by December, which satisfies the rest requirements of most of my plants. In January I begin to increase the duration again, until it is about fourteen hours by April. All lighting is controlled by a time clock. This change in photoperiodism has several interesting effects. Barbados-cherry (*Malpighia glabra*) begins to flower as the light is increased as does the dwarf pomegranate (*Punica granatum nana*) and some azaleas. Many other plants show no apparent response.

The Catlin elm (*Ulmus parvifolia* 'Catlin'), which is of borderline hardiness outdoors in New York, usually undergoes a brief rest period before being brought into the house. It takes approximately one month for this dwarf cultivar to resume growth and it does not start to leaf out well until the light duration is increased. Certain kinds of plants which are not normally thought of as indoor material can be grown under this system with the reduction of the night temperature to 55° F. They include *Juniperus procumbens 'Nana'*, Monterey cypress (*Cupressus macrocarpa*) and *Chamaecyparis thyoides 'Andelyensis'*. My giant-sequoia is surviving as are the live and scrub oaks of California. Azaleas and gardenias seem to do well but require a greater amount of humidity.

After thirty years of growing bonsai, I am enjoying them now more than ever. Which species survive under which conditions is one of the more interesting things I am now discovering. Growing bonsai indoors is a continual learning experience—one that is well worth the time and effort.

Climate makes a difference . . .

REPORT FROM
THE PACIFIC NORTHWEST

Jane Nelson

IN THE PACIFIC Northwest, particularly the Seattle area, indoor bonsai have not been as popular as in other parts of the United States. Our mild winters, cool summers, pure water and clean air are all factors in the continuing popularity of traditional bonsai. We can view the cool-climate bonsai favored by the Japanese, such as the spruces, pines and maples, through our windows as they sit outdoors on benches all winter. Only a few of them need a cold frame or a covering for a day or two. If one of these bonsai is moved inside for a short time, there are usually few problems because temperatures in the home are seldom more than twenty or twenty-five degrees different from outdoors.

New Favorites

Still, indoor bonsai are grown—by apartment dwellers and people like ourselves who enjoy experimenting with different plants. The small-leaved subtropical evergreens are favored. The most popular is serissa (*S. foetida*), also its variant with yellow leaf margins (*S. f. variegata*). This small shrub from Southeastern Asia is esteemed for its refined small white flowers and tiny foliage. Plants must be kept fairly close to a window for light because our gray winter days encourage legginess. The light intensity in the cold months is not sufficient for the flowering of some kinds of plants and we must occasionally supplement natural light with artificial.

The second most popular indoor bonsai in the Seattle area is the dwarf pomegranate (*Punica granatum nana*), which has narrow, lustrous, not-quite-evergreen leaves, scarlet flowers and reddish-orange fruit. A close third is New Zealand-tea (*Leptospermum scoparium*). It is a newcomer as a bonsai here but has been widely grown as an outdoor shrub in southern California, where numerous cultivars with single or double, pink to white flowers are available. We usually keep plants in an area with humidity—kitchen, bathroom, or on a saucer of pebbles with water.

Other plants are used, including false-heather (*Cuphea hyssopifolia*), correa (*C. magnifica*) and evergreen elm (*Ulmus parvifolia sempervirens*), which is not a subtropical but can take indoor conditions. Correa has been used successfully in a greenhouse but if treated as a bog plant performs very nicely inside the house in winter. Other people who have grown correa submerge the pots in water about once a month and give surface waterings in-between. One of the dwarf Natal-plums (*Carissa grandiflora* 'Nana Compacta') is used indoors, but its stiffness makes it less popular as a bonsai.

Less commonly mentioned but very successful are a South African succulent called elephant-bush (*Portulacaria afra*) and two myrtles (*Myrtus communis, M. ugni*). Their leaves are in good proportion to branch and trunk sizes. *Corokia cotoneaster*, a shrubby member of the Dogwood Family from New Zealand with twisting branches and small yellow star-like flowers, is also used for indoor bonsai, but the room temperature must be on the colder side.

Care and Soil

Fertilizing, pruning and general care of subtropical bonsai are the same as in other parts of the country. If possible, we put our plants outdoors in late May well after the last frost and bring them in again

63

Dwarf pomegranate, informal upright
style. One fruit is enough.

Arthur Orans

in late September before cool weather
begins. As elsewhere, gradual acclimation
is wise.

For potting, instead of relying on garden soil, which must then be pasteurized
in an oven, most people find it easier to
buy a pasteurized commercial three-way
mix from a garden center or nursery. To
this mix, the contents of which are
labeled sandy loam, compost and peat
moss, additional sand is incorporated by
the bonsai grower. The amount depends
on the texture of the mix, for some are
looser than others.

Even Bonsai Growers Need a Vacation

BECAUSE bonsai are grown in small containers, they require more frequent
watering than many house plants do, and the grower must be ever alert to their
needs. But what happens when *you* want a vacation? Try the "bonsai-sitter bag."
It's also an aid for acclimating plants newly purchased from a greenhouse or to
nurse recently root-pruned bonsai through a critical period. Here's how it works:
Use a clear plastic bag large enough to envelop the plant and container. Care
is essentially the same as for a terrarium. Water the soil well and let it drain
thoroughly before placing container in the bag. Make a "bubble" so bag doesn't
touch and rot foliage. The bag may have to be opened occasionally to allow
excess moisture to evaporate. This works well for about two weeks, and no
water will likely have to be added during this time. Open bag gradually over
several days to acclimate the plant to drier surroundings. Form wire into hoops
and insert into container to make a frame over the plant to support the
plastic.—*Edmond O. Moulin*

Adapt these ideas from Florida
for indoor use . . .

NOTES ON GROWING BONSAI
IN THE DEEP SOUTH

Winifred Glover and Virginia Harvey

Bougainvillea spp.—Keep plants relatively dry. Use a low-nitrogen fertilizer.

Dwarf Black-olive (*Bucida spinosa*)—Repotting here in Florida is best done in midsummer though possible in February. Use 7-8-4 fertilizer, not a high-nitrogen one that will encourage legginess. If seedlings are collected from the wild, cut the taproot when young.

Kingsville Dwarf Box (*Buxus microphylla* 'Compacta')—In our experience a loose, sandy soil mix is best. Rooted cuttings seem adapted to heat; our parent plant died.

Common Box (*Buxus sempervirens*)—It burns in full sun. Best kept moderately dry. Few pests here.

Dwarf Powder-puff (*Calliandra emarginata*)—Better for bonsai than the non-dwarf species because of smaller leaves and internodes. The spindly trunk is difficult to thicken.

Natal-plum (*Carissa grandiflora*)—Repotting in summer is safer than in spring. Use a deeper-than-usual pot for cool roots. Do not overwater because the old bark will rot. Edible fruit.

Citrus (Calamondin, Meyer lemon, kumquat, etc.) — Spray often for insects.

Dwarf black-olive (*Bucida spinosa*), 20 inches tall, 30 inches wide. Grown in container for 5 years, it requires little pinching to retain good form.

Peter Chvany

65

Sea-grape (*Coccoloba uvifera*)—Foliage is abnormally large for bonsai. Remove leaves (but not petioles) twice a year to control their size. For alkaline soil.

Buttonwood (*Conocarpus erectus*)—Plants collected from the wild lose their "salt-water" leaves; new ones have a different texture. Pinch back to two leaves.

Strangler Fig (*Ficus aurea*)—Growth slows after potting. Leaf size becomes very much smaller.

Weeping Fig (*Ficus benjamina*)—Don't spray with malathion. Plant will eventually form aerial roots.

Willow-leaved Fig (*Ficus neriifolia regularis*)—Drops leaves with sudden change in temperature but will adapt to air-conditioning if done gradually. Keep fairly dry until leaves return.

Hibiscus ('Snow Queen' and other small-flowered tropical varieties of *H. rosa-sinensis*)—Develops surface roots. Slow growing when established. In our experience plants have lived only seven or eight years.

Junipers (*Juniperus* spp.)—Necessary to spray frequently for mites here.

Upright Lantana (*Lantana camara*)—This is a weed here, easily gathered by uprooting, defoliating and placing in a paper bag. Watch for fungus infestations. Shape by pruning, not wiring, since branches are brittle.

Barbados-cherry (*Malpighia glabra*)—Must be grown in a large container to thicken trunk. Bears edible fruit if pollinated. Will drop all its leaves and grow new ones.

Cajeput-tree (*Melaleuca quinquenervia;* synonym, *M. leucadendron*)—Stands very hard root and top pruning. New growth will develop along the trunk. The attractive flaking bark of this Australian species has sparked a number of common names, including paperbark-tree, punk-tree and cork-tree.

Jaboticaba (*Myrciaria cauliflora*)—Requires acid soil and part shade. Leaf tips may scorch. Seeds sprout easily but it may take fifteen years before the edible fruit appears. Stewartia-like bark. Needs sun for fruiting.

Slash Pine (*Pinus elliottii*)—This two- or three-needle pine is native here. Cut taproot gradually if it has one. Provide well-drained soil. The needles, rather long for bonsai, are reduced by culture.

Philip B. Mullan

Strawberry-guava (*Psidium cattleianum*), slanting style. Bark becomes smooth with age, reminding a Japanese grower of Saru-suberi, the monkey-sliding tree, better known to westerners as crape-myrtle.

New growth breaks from old wood.

Ebony (*Pithecellobium brevifolium*)—Growth almost stops when container is too small. Shape it by pruning.

Strawberry Guava (*Psidium cattleianum*)—Especially recommended for its interesting trunk with mottled and peeling bark. Can be raised from seed. It grows rapidly, flowers at a fairly early stage and has edible red fruit.

Dwarf Pomegranate (*Punica granatum nana*)—Avoid wetting flowers if fruit is desired.

Serissa (*Serissa foetida*)—Blossoms well. It's difficult to develop a large trunk. Pinch new growth. Don't overfertilize.

Chinese Box-orange (*Severinia buxifolia*)—Be careful when pruning for shaping because branches are brittle.

Bald-cypress (*Taxodium distichum*)—Collect this well-known deciduous conifer of southern swamps only when it is dormant; prune tops and roots well at this time. In our experience subsequent pruning should be light—and not every year.

Limeberry (*Triphasia triphylla*)—Grows easily from seed or cuttings. Keep plants warm and well watered. A jelly is made from the fruit.

Evergreen Elm (*Ulmus parvifolia sempervirens*)—This variant of the Chinese elm seems to have no problems here. It can be fairly wet or dry, in full sun or light shade.

Bird Grape (*Vitis munsoniana*)—A native grape, easy to collect and grow. It's vigorous, so keep it pinched back.

Final note: To encourage moss we place cheesecloth on the soil around the bonsai. This material eventually disintegrates but in the meantime provides a good environment for moss to appear spontaneously. Also, we like the slow-release fertilizers. The nutrients are made available depending on amount of rainfall or watering.

Bonsai Materials from BBG

IF you are new to the ancient art of bonsai, there are two other Brooklyn Botanic Garden Handbooks to help you. *Bonsai—The Dwarfed Potted Trees of Japan* (No. 13 in our series) is a nitty-gritty introduction with fifteen articles by leading Japanese authorities. As in other BBG Handbooks, the stress is on how-to information that the home grower can put to work. *Bonsai—Special Techniques* (No. 51) elaborates on the essential points of culture, including how to prune and wire, and winter care of plants. Both Handbooks guest edited by Mr. Kan Yashiroda of Japan, are available for $4.75 a copy from Brooklyn Botanic Garden, 1000 Washington Ave., Brooklyn, N.Y. 11225.

There is a 21-minute BBG color film you should know about, too: *Bonsai*, in which the art of training dwarfed potted trees is beautifully depicted. It is available for rental or purhase and is ideal for plant society or garden club programs. Contact Brooklyn Botanic Garden Auxiliary for details. Same address as above.

Another color film that may be of particular interest though itdoes not deal directly with bonsai is *Pruning Practices at the Brooklyn Botanic Garden*. It runs 22 minutes and has a segment on the Japanese art of shape and form. Techniques for pruning the major groups of woody ornamental plants are also shown. Address as above.

Personal experiences with . . .

INDOOR BONSAI IN SOUTH FLORIDA
Virginia Nichols

INDOOR BONSAI are a great pleasure. Unlike the traditional kinds, they are cared for in the home year round, and the grower lives with them on a day-by-day basis. In time they become almost as much a part of the household as the family.

Air-Conditioned Bonsai

My own collection, which is kept on two tiers of glass shelves in front of a window, is not only an indoor collection but an air-conditioned one as well. Other southern gardeners who live under similar conditions need not be discouraged from growing bonsai for fear of the deleterious effects of air-conditioning. There are many plants that will not only live but thrive in this environment.

Because my apartment is centrally air-conditioned twenty-four hours a day, the windows are never opened. The window on which the bonsai are grouped faces west and is in a direct line with the air-conditioning duct 15 feet away. This is a safe distance; if any closer, difficulties may be encountered. My bonsai, which number between thirty and thirty-five, have survived nearly two-and-a-half years in this environment. The few that have succumbed in the interim have died from overwatering, incorrect soil mixes, spider mites and insufficient root systems. None died as a result of being indoors or from exposure to air-conditioning.

Heat and Water

Temperature in the window area, especially in southern climates where hot, sunny weather predominates, must be kept from becoming too high. Morning temperatures are usually no problem. In late afternoon, however, when the sun is at its strongest in my bonsai window, I simply draw a sheer drape across the window. This alleviates the intense heat and seems to prevent burning. A small thermometer sits on one shelf and the readings are surprisingly constant, rarely dipping below 73° or above 76°. On the rare occasions in winter when it turns cold enough for the heat to go on, I change nothing except to check more often to see if additional watering or misting is needed.

Watering indoor bonsai is no more difficult than watering outdoor bonsai. As a matter of fact, indoor bonsai require far less. Because of their protected location they are not exposed to the drying effects of direct sun and wind. Larger bonsai will benefit from being outdoors during *gentle* rains, but smaller ones that might blow over are best left indoors and misted instead.

My bonsai are watered nearly every morning with either purified water or tap water that has stood at room temperature for a day or two. An old detergent squeeze bottle serves well in lieu of a watering can, for I can regulate the amount of water better. A friend of mine likes to occasionally submerge her containers in water to just above the soil line. The bonsai remain under water until bubbles cease ascending. If this method is used, most bonsai, depending upon size, can go several days without water if not sensitive to low aeration in the soil.

My bonsai are watered lightly again before dusk. I first mist the soil surface—one quick spray on the mame and several more squirts on the rest. Each shelf-ful then gets its foliage misted briefly. Watering the plants in the home has the added advantage of being more gentle on the soil. Letting the rain water take care of outdoor plants is more apt to be violent in Florida because frequent downpours can disturb the soil and stain the pots. I fertilize actively growing plants once every three weeks, in the morning, applying a water-soluble fertilizer at half strength.

Philip B. Mullan

Parsley-aralia (*Polyscias fruticosa* 'Elegans'), 12 years old, 5 years in training.

Favored Plants

Throughout this Handbook there are recommendations for plant material suitable for indoor bonsai. The following suggestions are based on plants that have done well for me in Florida. *Ficus* (particularly *F. neriifolia regularis*) are exceptional, as is Norfolk Island-pine (*Araucaria heterophylla;* synonym, *A. excelsa*). The very pretty *Malpighia punicifolia* performs just as nicely indoors as it did for four years outside, and holly-leaved malpighia (*M. coccigera*) seems to flourish. Bougainvillea is excellent although its green coloring is not as dark as it should be. With the addition of trace elements, it may green up. One of my most interesting indoor bonsai is a *Polyscias*. Though not liked by all bonsai enthusiasts, it has proved most satisfactory for me. It requires comparatively little water, is not much affected by pests, stays green and healthy and can be styled to fit almost any spot. In addition, there are many varieties available to choose from.

A friend and I are both trying our luck indoors with sea-grape (*Coccoloba uvifera*). Mine is only 3¼ inches tall and has about thirteen leaves, the largest of which is 1¼ inches in diameter. This is an excellent leaf size for a potential bonsai. In the garden the leaves of this bold foliage plant are generally as much as 8 inches across. The fact that they do become small with bonsai culture is heartening. Thus far, our sea-grapes are only about ten months old so it's still too early to tell how they'll do as bonsai. At this point, however, both look good. Mistletoe fig (*Ficus diversifolia*) has always proven reliable for me as has the powder-puff (*Calliandra haematocephala*).

One bonsai which did very poorly indoors was a very small-leaved form of the Chinese elm, *Ulmus parvifolia* 'Catlin'. It was just a rooted cutting when brought into the home. I put it in a bonsai container much larger than needed, giving it sufficient room to grow. In two years time, during which it was repotted once, the Catlin elm failed to grow a single additional leaf. Three months ago I put it outdoors again, where it is once again thriving. In three months time I had to trim it twice!

Decorative Elements

Indoor bonsai have advantages over outdoor bonsai as decorative elements in the

69

home. One of mine sits in the center of a large round coffee-table in the den. It is flanked by a bronze statue of Diana and always looks pleasing. An 18-inch-tall ficus, it gets a small amount of water daily under my conditions of a cool air-conditioned room. Too much sun is not a problem as the table is about 12 feet from the window. Family and friends spend a great deal of time in this room and we all derive quiet pleasure from the bonsai's presence.

No matter where you choose to keep your bonsai indoors, one should always grace the dining-room table. I have an ixora on mine, and although there is a definite front and back, it seems to look right from most any angle. It is not very tall and usually has a few tiny bright red blossoms on display. It gives me special pleasure to use this as a centerpiece when

I entertain and it seems to be a great conversation piece among my guests.

Indoor bonsai are finally catching on and nothing could be a more welcome trend. In the South, they require little care and are constant sources of pleasure. Because most southern bonsai are subtropicals, they require a great deal of light, but this is easily arranged in Florida. Most homes here are built with large windows, sliding glass doors and white walls—all light enhancers.

I began by saying that indoor bonsai are a great pleasure and I hope you have become convinced. Why not try it yourself? You may lose some along the way, but experimentation is part of the fun. You'll soon find plants that will thrive in your conditions. When that happens you'll begin to enjoy the fruits of your labors and the admiration of your friends.

Malpighia punicifolia planted over rock displays natural root growth. Tree is about 9 inches tall.

Peter Chvany

Ficus and other plants for . . .

INDOOR BONSAI IN HAWAII

David Fukumoto

BONSAI are grown mainly outdoors year round in Hawaii. However, indoor bonsai are becoming increasingly popular as yards get smaller and more people move to townhouses and apartments. With the exception of dry heated air, we face the same problems of inadequate light, cultural adaptations and acclimation that growers do in other parts of the United States. In general, more glass is used in typical Hawaiian structures, but there is a movement toward artificial supplementary lighting when nesessary or for superior growth.

Indoor bonsai vary from simple attempts of tropical foliage plants in a bonsai pot to advanced bonsai designs. Initial attempts with common and durable house plants such as schefflera (*Brassaia*), pachira and polyscias are usually successful and pave the way toward more challenging plants. Because of larger leaves and non-woody trunks, they are often passed over for bonsai. However, bonsai techniques will produce striking designs and provide easy-care indoor showpieces.

The Old Trees

A bonsai grower with a little experience uses tropical plants that have woody trunks. The major plants in this category are Chinese banyan (*Ficus retusa*) and weeping fig (*F. benjamina*). Although they are related, growth and training vary considerably. Whereas weeping fig must be propagated from cuttings, Chinese banyan has fertile seeds and volunteer seedlings can be collected from rocks, walls, rain gutters, sidewalk cracks and on host trees. There are many fine mature trees of Chinese banyan with amazing aerial root systems here. Even weeping fig will form aerial roots under heavy leaf canopy and high humidity.

With or without aerial roots, the *Ficus* species have impressive shapes. A *Ficus elastica* planted in Hilo in the 1870's has formed a multi-trunked tree with a lofty crown and huge buttressing roots. With maturity the leaf size has been naturally reduced to only a few inches and upon seeing the tree for the first time it's unthinkable that it's the same as the popular indoor "rubber tree." The massive form of this and many other large ficus trees in Hawaii serves as inspiration for tropical bonsai.

Fuku-Bonsai

Australian brush-cherry (*Syzygium paniculatum*, but often sold as *Eugenia myrtifolia*) is a good beginner's bonsai. This plant is 15 inches tall.

Fuku-Bonsai

Collected plant of Chinese banyan (*Ficus retusa*) being trained on lava rock. It displays aerial roots typical of mature trees of this type.

Most warm-climate trees have large leaves but if their foliage is removed two to four times per year, leaf size is reduced drastically. Remove by stripping, except for the Sea-grape, which must be cut in a manner that leaves the petioles attached. Smaller-leaved trees available for indoor bonsai include citrus, eugenia, jaboticaba, melaleuca, olive, podocarpus and pomegranate. Shrubs include bougainvillea, carissa, lantana, malpighia and serissa. In almost every advanced collection others are being tried that would be suitable for indoor bonsai.

Although mild-climate plants are mentioned above, the possibilities for indoor bonsai include a few kinds from cooler areas. Initial trials indicate that pyracantha, evergreen azaleas, cryptomeria, cupressus and chamaecyparis will do well indoors. Plants that elongate and become spindly in semi-shade are ruled out.

Light Factors and Styling

Some plants acclimate well to indoors directly from full sun, but most will benefit by an intermediate period in shade. Plants should not be growing vigorously and should be leached of fertilizer by soaking, flushing or scraping the salts off the pot rim before coming indoors. Plants grow in relationship to their light availability; and since indoor light in Hawaii is often one tenth or less of outdoors, fertilizing and watering needs are less also. Good drainage, moisture and watering practices are more important indoors. Because the indoor bonsai are getting attention more often, initial attempts usually fail by killing them with kindness.

Styling of indoor bonsai tends to be more subtle and not as dramatic as the traditional evergreen bonsai. In finding design inspiration from the mature tropical trees we find a preponderance of heavy rounded crowns and arching branches rather than the traditional tier-branching. Exposed roots are often more dramatic and barks more varied. A number of warm-climate plants have flowers that bloom throughout the year.

In selecting plants for indoor bonsai consideration should be given to differences in plant growth under indoor and outdoor growing conditions. In Hawaii the two most popular outdoor bonsai plants are the Japanese black pine (*Pinus thunbergii*) and Australian-ironwood (*Casuarina* spp.). Both are highly variable when grown from seed. Both tend to become spindly when shade grown indoors, and an extraordinary amount of artificial light is needed to supplement even the brightest light indoors if they are to perform well.

Experiments

We do many trials to select outstanding candidates for indoor bonsai that are smaller-leaved and naturally compact. With highly variable species many variants are tested; and if one clone proves to be superior, other trial plants are discarded and the superior clone propagated asexually by cuttings. Occasionally, a branch mutation appears with dwarf leaves and compact branches. This is air-layered and serves as a stock plant. Sometimes plants propagated from cuttings are superior to plants grown from seed. In other cases the reverse is true.

Over the years that traditional bonsai has developed in the Orient, many of the plants most popular and suitable have been propagated and introduced to their bonsai community in this painstaking manner.

Indoor bonsai is very much in the pioneering stage, but the active search and discovery of outstanding and suitable plants have progressed well. Whereas traditional bonsai developed in the Orient under very secretive conditions, indoor bonsai is progressing rapidly because of plants of faster growth and cooperation between growers in all parts of the country. Nursery certification programs are lowering plant distribution barriers that once made plant movement difficult between states. New techniques and available aids make re-establishment of plant stock less of a gamble even when a plant has been bare-rooted and fumigated. New methods of packing and use of air services get plants to destinations in prime condition. All of this hastens the day

Indoor bonsai in training in Hawaii. From left: schefflera, serissa, dwarf azalea, schefflera, golden Sawara false-cypress (*Chamaecyparis pisifera* 'Aurea'). The tallest is 10 inches.

Fuku-Bonsai

73

when superior plant material will become available to anyone interested in indoor bonsai.

Once plants are selected and indoor cultural procedures are learned, there is little difference between indoor and outdoor bonsai. At first miniature bonsai were difficult, as we tended to overwater them. Now complete assembled miniature landscapes do well indoors. Rock plantings are easier indoors because they drain well and don't dry out so quickly.

Smaller bonsai benefit from easily improvised supplemental artificial light. Larger bonsai require more elaborate lighting arrangements.

We're fortunate in Hawaii to have a store of basic bonsai knowledge, suitable plant material and an even and mild climate. With these basic advantages, both indoor and outdoor bonsai have increasingly brought joy and fulfillment to those who take up this fascinating pastime.

ACKNOWLEDGMENTS:

All photographs by Peter Chvany are courtesy of the Arnold Arboretum, Jamaica Plain, Massachusetts. A special word of appreciation is due Margo W. Reynolds, Arnold Arboretum, who served as assistant to Guest Editor Derderian. Several people graciously made available their bonsai for photographing. They include Elinor Fallon, Marblehead, Massachusetts, Elma Berryman, Ft. Lauderdale, Florida and Olivia Holmes, Chestnut Hill, Massachusetts.

Plants From A to Z,
nt. from p. 59).

drier winter than summer to lose its leaves. During the surge of new growth in spring, give plant plenty of water.
Trachelospermum jasminoides—Confederate-jasmine, Star-jasmine. (1). Be sure to pinch the strong-vining new growth of this twining shrub from the Himalayas. The white flowers are deliciously fragrant and the leathery foliage is always attractive.
Ulmus parvifolia sempervirens—Evergreen Elm. (1). See page 67. Excellent for very small or shallow containers.

Wisteria spp. (4). For the keen bonsai enthusiast, this well-known vine is a challenge in the home. It's worth the extra effort to produce the bloom. Excellent light is needed, plus careful pruning.
Xylosma bahamensis. (1-3). Caribbean tree with silver-gray bark and very graceful, feathery leaves. It's fast growing—watch for wire cuts. Responds well to pruning.
Ziziphus jujuba—Jujube, Chinese-date. (2-3). Small tree with dense lustrous foliage. Hardy in the North but grown mostly in mild climates. Tolerant of alkaline soil. The small light-brown edible fruits are not very ornamental in the garden but have a certain charm when jujube is grown as a bonsai.

INDEX

Acacia baileyana, 50
  farnesiana, 50
Aeonium domesticum, 48
Aloysia triphylla, 47
Aralia, Finger-, 7
Araucaria bidwillii, 7
  excelsa, see
    heterophylla
  heterophylla, 50, 69
Azalea, 35, 37, 59, 62, 72

Banyan, Chinese, 42, 71
Bay, 56
Beech, Tasmanian-, 57, 58
Bougainvillea, 35, 37, 50, 65, 69, 72
Box, Boxwood, 35, 38, 39, 47, 50, 51, 65
Box, African-, 57
Box, Kingsville Dwarf, 38, 39, 51, 65
Brassaia actinophylla, 7, 71
Bucida buceras, 50
  spinosa, 50, 65
Bursera simaruba, 50
Buttonwood, 52, 66
Buxus harlandii, 50
  microphylla, 35, 51
  microphylla 'Compacta', 38, 39, 51, 65
  sempervirens, 39, 47, 65

Cajeput-tree, 66
Calliandra emarginata, 14, 51, 65
  haematocephala, 51, 69
  inaequilatera, see
    haematocephala
  surinamensis, 51
Camellia, 35, 40, 51
Camphor-tree, 51
Carissa grandiflora, 35, 51, 63, 65, 72
  grandiflora 'Nana Compacta', 63
Cassia marilandica, 51
Casuarina, 72
Cat's Claw, 58
Chaenomeles japonica, 51
Chamaecyparis, 35, 51, 62, 72
  pisifera 'Plumosa', 51
  pisifera 'Squarrosa', 51
  thyoides 'Andelyensis', 62
Cherry, Barbados-, 37, 57, 62, 66
Cherry, Brush-, 14, 35
Cherry, Surinam-, 53
Cinnamomum camphora, 51
Cissus rhombifolia, 52
Citrus, 7, 47, 52, 65
Clerodendrum thom-

  soniae, 52
Coccoloba uvifera, 52, 66, 69
Conocarpus erectus, 52, 66
Corokia cotoneaster, 63
Correa magnifica, 63
Cotoneaster, 52
Crassula, 7, 49
  argentea, 7
Cryptomeria japonica, 52, 72
Cuphea hyssopifolia, 52, 63
Cupressus arizonica, 8, 53
  macrocarpa, 8, 53, 62
Cycas revoluta, 8
Cypress, 8, 53, 72
Cypress, Bald-, 67, 75
  Moss-, 51
  Plume-, 51

Date, Chinese-, 75
Distylium racemosum, 53
Dizygotheca elegantissima, 7

Ebony, 67
Elephant-bush, 49, 63
Elm, Chinese and Evergreen, 35, 63, 67, 69, 75

75

Eugenia myrtifolia, see
  Syzygium
  paniculata, see
  Syzygium
  uniflora, 53
Eurya japonica, 53

Faith-tree, 51
Ficus aurea, 8, 53, 66
  benjamina, 35, 54, 66,
    71
  diversifolia, 54, 69
  elastica, 71
  neriifolia regularis, 35,
    42, 54, 66, 68
  pumila, 35
  pumila minima, 54
  retusa, 42, 71
  retusa nitida, 54
Fig, Creeping, 35, 54
  Mistletoe, 54, 69
  Strangler, 8, 53, 66
  Weeping, 35, 54, 66, 71
  Willow-leaved, 35, 42,
    54, 66, 68
Firethorn, 35, 58, 72
Fortunella hindsii, 54

Gardenia jasminoides, 8,
  37, 62
  jasminoides radicans,
    35, 40, 41, 55
Geometry-tree, 50
Geranium, 48
Geranium, Jungle-, 55
Germander, 47
Glorybower, 52
Grape, Bird, 67
Grape, Sea-, 52, 66, 69
Grevillea robusta, 54
Guaiacum officinale, 54
Guava, Strawberry-, 58,
  67
Gumbo Limbo, 50

Hawthorn, India-, 59
Heather, False-, 52, 63
Hedera helix, 35, 47, 55
Hemp, African-, 59
Hibiscus, 35, 55, 66
Holly, English, 47, 55
  Japanese, 55
  Yaupon, 55
  Singapore-, 1, 57, 60, 69
Holywood, 54
Honeysuckle, Box, 57

Ilex aquifolium, 47, 55
  aquifolium 'Angus-
    tifolia', 55
  crenata 'Helleri', 55

  crenata 'Microphylla',
    55
  vomitoria, 55
  vomitoria 'Stokes
    Dwarf', 55
Ironwood, Australian-, 72
Ivy, English, 35, 47
Ivy, Grape-, 52
Ixora javanica, 55
  javanica 'Nor-nel', 55

Jaboticaba, 6, 72
Jacaranda, 55
Jade Plant, 7
Jasmine, Confederate-, 14,
  75
  Pinwheel, 55
  Star-, 75
Jasminum dichotomum, 55
  rex, 55
Jujube, 75
Juniperus chinensis 'San
  José', 8
  chinensis sargentii, 56
  procumbens 'Nana', 55,
    62
  squamata 'Prostrata', 56

Kumquat, Wild, 54

Lagerstroemia indica, 56
Lantana, 35, 56, 66, 72
Laurus nobilis, 56
Lavandula, 47
Lavender, 47
Leptospermum scoparium,
  56, 63
Lignum Vitae, 54
Ligustrum japonicum, 56,
  57
  japonicum 'Rotundifoli-
    um', 57
  lucidum, 57
Limeberry, 35, 67
Lippia citriodora, see
  Aloysia
Lonicera nitida, 57

Malpighia coccigera, 1,
  57, 60, 69, 72
  glabra, 57, 62, 66
  punicifolia, 35, 57, 69
Melaleuca leucadendron,
  66
  quinquenervia, 66
Mimosa, 50
Myrciaria cauliflora, 66
Myrsine africana, 57
Myrtle, 44-47, 57, 63
Myrtle, Crape-, 56

Myrtus communis, 44,
  57, 63
  ugni, 63

Nicodemia diversifolia, 7,
  57
Nothofagus cunninghamii,
  57, 58

Oaks, 58, 59, 62
Oak, Indoor-, 7, 57
Oak, Silk-, 54
Olea europaea, 8, 35, 47,
  58
Olive, 8, 35, 47, 58
Olive, Black-, 50
Olive, Dwarf Black-, 50,
  65
Olive, Sweet-, 47
Orange, Box-, 67
Osmanthus fragrans, 47

Pachira, 71
Palm, Sago-, 8
Pine, Aleppo, 58
  Japanese Black, 58, 72
  Norfolk Island-, 50, 69
  Slash, 66
Pinus elliotii, 66
  halepensis, 58
  thunbergii, 58, 72
Pithecellobium bre-
    vifolium, 67
  unguis-cati, 58
Pittosporum tobira, 7, 58
Plum, Natal-, 35, 51, 63,
  65
Podocarpus macrophyllus,
  8, 58
Polyscias, 69
Pomegranate, Dwarf, 35,
  58, 62, 63, 67, 72
Portulacaria afra, 49, 63
Powder-puff, 14, 51, 65, 69
Privet, 56, 57
Psidium cattleianum, 58,
  67
Punica granatum nana,
  35, 58, 62, 63, 67
Pyracantha species, 35,
  58, 72
  angustifolia, 58
  coccinea, 58
  fortuneana, 58
  koidzumii, 58

Quercus species, 58, 59,
  62
  agrifolia, 59
  nigra, 59
  suber, 59